"Revelations from the Light: What I Learned about Life's Purposes brings a fresh and exciting perspective to understanding the spiritual messages of near-death experiences. Everyone can benefit from learning the wisdom so clearly and eloquently expressed in this book. With each turn of the page you will find a treasure trove of insights, inspiration, and practical pointers that will *really* work in your life. This outstanding book is expertly written, remarkably easy to read, and enthusiastically recommended."

—Jeffrey Long, M.D., author of the New York Times bestselling *Evidence of the Afterlife: The Science of Near-Death Experiences*, and *God and the Afterlife: The Groundbreaking New Evidence for God and Near-Death Experience*

"In *Revelations from the Light: What I Learned about Life's Purposes*, Nancy Clark writes, "At the heart of humanity there is a deep yearning to know God." With this truth deeply embedded in each of our souls, I believe Nancy's book empowers all of us to refocus our lives on that which is truly important: finding and expressing the Divine. Through her NDE and NDE-like experiences, Nancy discovered this timeless wisdom and through her book, she is offering the entire world this precious gift."

—Dannion Brinkley, New York Times bestselling author of *Saved by the Light*, CEO, The Twilight Brigade

"Nancy Clark's near-death and near-death-like experiences offer profound insights into the nature, origin and destiny of consciousness. Of the 15 million Americans who profess near-death experiences, I know of no one whose experience exceeds the richness of Nancy's recurrent encounters with the Transcendent. *Revelations from the Light* explains why."

—Larry Dossey, M.D., New York Times bestselling author: *One Mind: How our Individual Mind is Part of a Greater Consciousness and Why It Matters*

"Many people feel that they have had an encounter with God during their near-death experiences, but few return with a sense of divinely sanctioned mission to speak God's truth about how we are meant to live in this world of ours. Nancy Clark is that rare soul who was "told" in no uncertain terms to write such a book, and *Revelations from the Light* is the book you now hold in your hands. In it, you will find the most important, God-inspired, lessons that Nancy has been able to extract from her own personal encounters with the divine."

—Kenneth Ring, Ph.D., Author of *Lessons from the Light*

"Ms. Clark's incredible experiences give life far more meaning than ever before. She inspires us all to love deeper, to reach further and be brighter in the sacred 'right now.' Her powerful realizations that the little things in life are actually the big things literally brings heaven to earth. The profound truth that we are all divine, and simply here on earth to love and take care of each other, is a message the world is aching for. A must read for anyone wanting to experience more Light."

—Jeff Olsen, Author of *I Knew Their Hearts and Beyond Mile Marker 80*

"Our world is already lighter and more enlightened thanks to all the energy and love in Nancy's latest book. Gaining the insights shared in *Revelations from the Light* could require countless time-space experiences here and in the hereafter. Or, you can benefit by reading and applying its wisdom now. Please share this inspiring and heart-expanding book with everyone you know!"

—Mark Pitstick, MA, DC, Author of *Soul Proof* and Director of Education for Eternea.org

"With heartfelt sincerity, Nancy Clark bares her soul as she shares the many lessons she learned through four incredible spiritually transformative experiences. She answers some of life's greatest questions including the meaning of life, the nature of God and the essence of the soul. No one can read this beautiful book without feeling the presence of the Divine and embracing the joyful knowledge that there truly is life after death."

—Josie Varga, Author of *A Call from Heaven, Divine Visits, Visits to Heaven* and *Visits from Heaven*

"In this book, Nancy Clark generously shares, selflessly, only what the Source inspires. I am a New Yorker, (natural born skeptics) and I want to come close to the Truth. As one who has not had an NDE, but as someone who researches NDEs so as to find and share the relief from the suffering, pain and fear in this life, Nancy's words are all the more credible as they are striped of glamour: egoless-words, shared as selfless service."

—Randy Klinger, NDE conference organizer and artist

"Books by and about people who have had spiritual experiences are everywhere these days. What separates Nancy's book from most others is that Nancy has spent DECADES attempting to understand and integrate her experiences. Which brings up a second point: she's also had four major spiritually transformative experiences (one classic near-death experience and three near-death-like experiences.) That's a potent combination. While spiritual experiences of all kinds have things to teach us, people who have spent a lifetime attempting to understand and ground their experiences bring a depth of understanding to the table when they've had multiple spiritually-transformative experiences and are attempting, every day, to apply the insights gleaned from these life-changing experiences to the challenges of everyday life.

Bottom line: this book is full of pearls of great price. It offers seasoned insights about the purpose of life, the transformative power of God's unconditional love, the challenging nature of the spiritual path, the need to listen to our own heart and follow our own path, the importance of paying attention to the little things in life, the power of prayer and dreams, and much more. I applaud Nancy for writing this book and, more importantly, living a life that brings universal truths alive."

—David Sunfellow, Author of *Love the Person You're With*

"For someone who claims she can't write, here's another homerun for Nancy Clark. It's different and it's a WOW! She hovers between the Great God of Light that fills her and the all-too-human grief that came when the love of her life died. She tells us about when she woke up in the morgue, a corpse-come-back-to-life, and about the sudden upliftment that came when Light engulfed her while she was delivering a eulogy at a friend's funeral. You get the very real sense that although Nancy is now God-infused through and through, her life is really one of simple pleasures. She has become what she writes about."

—P.M.H. Atwater, L.H.D., Researcher of near-death states, author of such books as, *Future Memory, The Big Book of Near-Death Experiences, Dying to Know You,* and *Near-Death Experiences: The Rest of the Story.* Her *A Manual for Developing Humans* is due out Spring, 2017.

"*In Revelations from the Light: What I Learned about Life's Purposes,* Nancy Clark brilliantly expresses her amazing personal experiences in the Light. While reading it, I had the feeling I was floating down a wonderful, beautiful stream – the stream of life – toward a bridge I would pass under – the bridge to the Light – and I would be prepared to cross. I very highly recommend this book. I predict that it will be a best seller."

—Vernon Sylvest, M.D., author of *The Formula: Who Gets Sick, Who Gets Well, Who is Unhappy, Who is Happy and Why*

REVELATIONS
FROM THE
LIGHT:

What I Learned About Life's Purposes

NANCY CLARK

Revelations from the Light: What I Learned About Life's Purposes

Nancy Clark

Published by 1st World Publishing
P.O. Box 2211, Fairfi eld, Iowa 52556
tel: 641-209-5000 • fax: 866-440-5234
web: www.1stworldpublishing.com

First Edition
LCCN: 2017902541
Softcover ISBN: 978-1-4218-3775-8

This material has been written and published for educational purposes to enhance one's well-being. In regard to health issues, the information is not intended as a substitute for appropriate care and advice from health professionals, nor does it equate to the assumption of medical or any other form of liability on the part of the publisher or author. The publisher and author shall have neither liability nor responsibility to any person or entity with respect to loss, damages, or injury claimed to be caused directly or indirectly by any information in this book.

DEDICATION

*"To Him who is able to do exceedingly abundantly above all
that we ask or think, according to the power that works in us,
to Him be the glory.*
Ephesians 3:20-21

I dedicate this book to my Great Teacher, the Light-God
who called me to serve in a way that I would never have
assumed on my own. God turned my life into a great
passage from life to death and back to life again so that I
could inspire others to learn how to manifest the Love and
the Beauty of the Divine, and that all may be lifted into a
greater awareness of their Divine Nature.

I have learned to completely trust God to help me fulfill
the purpose I was given. When I do this, the Light-God
invariably prepares the way for me, just as I was promised
during my near-death-like experience. It was a great moment
of beauty when the Light-God told me, "As long as you
hold onto My Hand and don't let go, I shall lead, you shall
follow. The path ahead of you shall be prepared for you."

I promised to serve. In so doing, I found that my calling
is not as impossible as I thought it might be. Yes, I was led

on a new path, and a new way of life to inspire others to be an expression of the Light in the world, but I am always reminded that it is the Divine Source in me who is the power who carries out the work through me. I will forever be indebted to the One who gifted me with this new life to be of service to others.

To my Great Teacher, the Light-God, I dedicate this book.

Thank you for helping me to write it. All glory be Thine.

ACKNOWLEDGMENTS

"God has not called us to see through each other,
but to see each other through."

—Unknown

This book is not a solitary effort even though I have written it. There are people behind the scenes who are responsible for the birthing of this book and I am grateful to them all.

To the prestigious authors who have endorsed my book and whose reputations lend credibility to my own work, thank you for helping to bring the Light's healing love to the world through your own works, and in mine as well. I offer a standing ovation to show how deeply grateful I am to the following people:

Dannion Brinkley; Jeffrey Long, M.D.; Larry Dossey, M.D.; Ken Ring, PhD; PMH Atwater, LHD; Vernon Sylvest, M.D., Josie Varga; Jeff Olsen; David Sunflower; Mark Pitstick, DC.; and Randy Klinger.

A hearty hug goes to Pat Stillisano, DDS who listened to the deepest part of my heart at times when I thought I was the only one on the planet who felt a certain way. His vast knowledge and years of studying mysticism and the saints gave me comfort in knowing that the deepest feelings in my heart were similarly being expressed by the saints. (No, I am **not** a saint; please don't get that impression.) But in patiently listening to me reflect unknowingly what the mystics and saints were also reporting about their experiences with God, Pat helped me immensely with the encouragement and support I was in need of. God bless you "Professor" Pat!

Others who deserve special recognition are friends who have been my collective support group over the years waiting for this book to be written. They are the following:

Bill Hoover, M.D., Jan Jurkuta, Mark Lutz, Randy Klinger, Bill Guggenheim, Joyce Gibb, RN, Rev. Bill McDonald, and members of my Columbus, Ohio IANDS group, (International Association for Near-Death Studies.) I would thank you from the bottom of my heart, but for you my heart has no bottom.

My computer guru friends, Jeff Lutz and Rick Fisher, who spent countless hours trying to repair the problems I encountered while working on my computer. You are a God-sent blessing to me! Seriously!

My cherished friend, Vernon Sylvest, M.D., sometimes I just wonder what I would have done without you. You have been the pillar I've been leaning on all these years. If I could give our friendship a name, it would be Memories Unlimited. Thanks for giving me beautiful memories that I am going to cherish for a lifetime, and for being the support system of my life.

In loving memory of Reverend Tsuneo Miyashiro and my mother, for sharing my dream so completely. My husband Ched who is now experiencing all I tried to tell him when he was still alive, that life exists after physical death. He didn't believe then, but now he knows. For giving me the balance in life that I needed, thank you Ched!

To my two sons Chris and Randy who became my rocks

after my husband died, giving me their unfailing love and support, making me the proudest and luckiest mom in the world.

I am sincerely grateful to my editors, Michael Hoover, and William Hoover, M.D. for all they have done for this book. It was obvious that they took great care to preserve my voice, and not to change meaning when structure needed adjusting. Thanks to them for a wonderful partnership!

I must acknowledge the loving support from my dear publisher, Rodney Charles, 1st World Publishing, who believed in the healing value of this book, and for making it a reality. What a warm and lovely person you are. It has been a privilege working with you and with your staff. A big bear hug to you, Rodney. God loves you, and so do I!

To the Source of Creation, I offer my gratitude every day!

CONTENTS

AUTHOR'S NOTE

Dear Reader,
You will notice that I use the word God in the masculine tense frequently throughout the book. I would encourage you to substitute whatever name you personally use, in accordance with your own belief system when referring to your Creator, Divine Source, or Higher Self.

INTRODUCTION

There comes a time in one's life when we get a glimpse of the purpose of our life. My time came when I was taken up into the Heavenly Realm with the Light-God in 1979 when I was given a calling at that time to "speak and write" what my Great Teacher, the Light-God revealed to me. Great knowledge and wisdom were brought into my midst with the understanding that I would return from Heaven's door so that others would be permitted to see and understand the Presence of the Beloved in physical life. With great love and my promise to God to fulfill my calling, I returned anxious to help others learn and understand their earth life and the work they may do to awaken to the joy of knowing one's True Self – their Divine Self.

I wrote the following email to a friend and realized I had written the introduction to my book. This is exactly what I told him and now I am telling you.

"So now I am going to expose my feeling about my book that I have been having ever since its inception.

First of all, you recall that God called me to 'speak and write' what He revealed to me and told me to tell everyone. I promised I would do that no matter what, and I have kept that promise.

What I experienced with God was so truthful in every respect that I would never lead anyone in the wrong direction with what I tell them.

My life review was very painful because when I was in that other dimension with God, I saw and understood everything in a different way than we see or understand things in this reality. It was crystal clear there because no ego was involved.

Having said that, I try my hardest to tell people that, and to inspire and encourage them to live a better life NOW – not wait until they get on the other side and then "get it" like I did.

I get so discouraged because I don't believe people are listening to this message. They read or listen to people who have been on the other side as if they want to be "entertained" by their stories. Nice story....but they go on with their lives hoping that when they die, they will experience the same love, beauty, etc. that they read or heard about.

But I've come back, with the Light's message to live NOW, growing in spiritual awareness. Especially that life review! Getting to experience the actual feelings that someone felt when that person did something bad to them, re-living that incident, moment to moment. Heck, I was shocked to learn that it also includes the very small things as well. Imagine feeling what someone felt like when that person was so happy about something – perhaps graduated with a special honor, and someone they were very close to never bothered to say congratulations, nice job, or something that would convey they were happy for the graduate. Imagine how disappointed and let down the graduate would feel. Well, during your life review, you would get to experience his disappointment. Or imagine the same thing for an employee who worked overtime without pay and who performed the work extremely well, but never received a compliment from his boss for a job well done. If you were his boss, you would get to experience that employee's feeling of being taken for granted. You would then understand how many opportunities were presented to you as the lessons to be learned during earth life and you failed to act upon them.

These incidents are small, and we tend not to think of them as hurtful or disappointing to anyone. But the bigger picture is that during our life review we get to see that incident in context of the larger, *Spiritual* picture, not the earthly one. And I can tell you, it is very, very painful.

So here I am, just one ordinary person who promised God during my experience that I would try and help others to "get this message" so they can live better lives NOW, and not have to find out later, that every single moment of their lives will be reviewed. Every thought and every action will be shown to the individual.

As I was working on my book, there were times when I got so sad because here I go again, trying to encourage people, knowing that they will probably read the book and say, "*That was a good book.*" Then they will go back to their ordinary lives and not take the message with them to prepare for those life reviews on the other side when they die.

At times I cried and cried and I wanted to quit writing – quit hoping that people will "get it." Sad because I know most people won't "get it" and begin changing their lives by giving compliments to others, acknowledging someone as being important to them, doing a little favor for someone, lifting someone up when they are sad with a simple hug. So many simple, little acts of kindness are HUGE, HUGE, HUGE when we get on the other side and we see how many opportunities came to us to express our true spiritual nature and we did not act. The regret we will feel is not like it is here. Over there, when we get to see and directly experience a much higher level of Spirit, those little tiny moments we failed to act lovingly will be extremely painful. **I don't want people to feel that regret!** But as I worked on my book, I felt like I was failing in some way. I felt no one would care enough to "get that message" **now**. I felt no one would understand the imperative to begin living from their Divine Nature, the reason we are here, living our earthly lives.

I struggled with this all throughout the writing process, but all the while, I felt the Presence of God Who I know was helping me to write this important book. I know and felt His support and encouragement to keep writing.

I still feel sort of sad about it. I guess I can't control others' feelings and behaviors, but I sure hope a few people will "get it" before their time runs out. I hope my book will be their "wake-up call."

1

WHY AND HOW THIS BOOK WAS WRITTEN

My Beloved,
Wait for me in everything. Your ego challenges you to act
on your own right now but you must be still and listen to
My Voice within before you act impulsively.

To be honest, I never had a desire to write books – ever, until one day by a completely unexpected and inexplicable experience, my Spirit-self was taken up into the Sacred Reality, "home" where I experienced union with God. There, within the rapture of the timelessness, the exquisite splendor, beauty and peace, the Light-God was being revealed to me like sunlight in a shady forest. This was a gift that changed me through love and humility, a gift beyond any and all possible merit, a gift of the most unspeakable Grace.

It was during my experience that I was instructed to "speak and write" what my Great Teacher, the Light-God, revealed to me. It was a "calling" to work with God to carry me beyond myself, beyond where I could or would choose to go on my own. I promised I would begin this new journey that ultimately would become my destiny. To become willing to be of service to God and to others, is my gift back to God for this loving opportunity to help others as I have been helped.

On my own, (my ordinary, waking consciousness), I cannot speak or write as poignantly as many of the words that appear in my books. Everything that is written is what I experienced with the Light-God. But sometimes I cannot consciously recall some knowledge I experienced. I have found however, that while being in a receptive frame of mind, and maintaining a listening ear in the inner stillness of my being, the information does surface while I am engaged in the writing process.

Writing does not come easily for me. It took several years before I was able to write my first book that the Light in-structed me to write. I wasn't successful because I was trying to control the writing process through my ego-self. It was a painstaking endeavor that I had never been prepared for. Besides, I never wrote anything except letters home to my parents. What did I know about writing a book? Nothing.

Dejected after months and years of trying to write my book, I began to feel that the Light-God had called the wrong person to write a book about the knowledge that I was supposed to communicate to the masses. I felt that I was forsaking the One who had gifted me. I could not write, and the more I tried, the more I failed.

One day, while trying to work on the book again, a sudden excruciating helplessness fell upon me. My senses were expressing the disappointment I felt in myself, and the disappointment I felt for not being able to serve God. My voice wailed out through my tears shouting,

"Why me, God? Why did you call me to write? I can't do this! **God, I can't do this!"**

By this time, an overwhelming outpouring of all the enthusiasm I had for fulfilling my calling left my mind, heart and soul. I felt stripped of any ability in my human body to write what God had instructed me to do. I was feeling adrift, like a raft that had lost its anchor.

Kneeling on the floor in what can only be described as complete emptying of my will, I cried out to God,

"You have to help me. I can't do this by myself. Please help me! You promised to help me, so I'm begging you now to help me write the book that you asked me to write."

I felt emotionally drained and exhausted. There were no more tears left to shed, no more words to speak. I had surrendered myself completely to God with not a smidgeon of ego remaining within me. It was now all up to God as to whether He would carry out His promise to help me with my calling.

Suddenly, an unearthly peace came over me. The peace began to flow through my body starting from my toes, traveling up my spine, and exiting from the top of my head. I knew at that moment that God had heard my cries. I knew at that moment that God wouldn't allow me to fail in the work He had called me to do.

With renewed faith and confidence, I immediately got up off the floor and went to my computer where a blank screen stared at me. Almost immediately, I felt words flowing through my consciousness, words I had not planned on writing. Like waves of a beautiful fragrance, the words drifted into my heart and mind. The feeling of God's actual presence with me was the feeling of having transcended the five physical senses. My intuitive faculty became receptive to the thoughts which came to me from within, and a stream of words began to flow.

The writing became effortless and I was finding great

joy in it, unlike the struggle I had felt previously. That experience taught me to put my ego-self on a shelf, out of the way when I want to write about the spiritual matters of my heart, and just allow Spirit within to inspire me. I learned that day to lower and humble myself to God, and allow God to use me in the way that God chooses. I had been letting my ego get in my way, blocking the connection to the Divine Presence within. That first book that I wrote with God's help, *Hear His Voice*, became a national award-winning book.

This book I have written is my fifth book. Each book was not written through a conscious reasoning process; rather, there was an intuitive, inner guidance that my Spirit was revealing to me what I needed to do. Apparently, God still wants me to continue writing and inspiring others, so I lovingly consent to continue this work.

Before I make the decision to write, I enter into a personal union with the Divine. I take about one half hour to center myself by praying and lifting my love to God. I am in tears by then, raising my love to such a level of sincerity that I cannot contain it in my physical body any longer. I am gushing with love and my tears are flowing like a river. I simply cannot hold one more ounce of love inside of me. Trusting that I will be led by God to do this work, I allow my love for God to replace my willfulness that was driving me to write on my own, and in that way love and humility become the initiators of my spiritual work.

It is then that I begin to feel an extraordinary intensity within my heart, which I can only describe as "feeling the Divine Presence." At that point I become a small child in my own eyes. I tell God that I don't have the foggiest idea what this book should be about, so I ask God to use me as I write so that my work for Him will be well served and help others in some way. Then I begin to write, most of the time not knowing what to write or how to write. I simply turn myself over to the Divine Presence within to guide my writing by the feelings that build up within me.

You could say that as I write, it is as if I "go to a different place" other than my ordinary physical consciousness to allow whatever wisdom that I am being led to write will be brought to the surface of my consciousness from my soul. I don't think that God gives me the exact words to write because I am still human and have some human filters to acknowledge, but the gist of the information is, in my opinion, spot-on.

I trust in this Divine process because on my own I could never write what I have written. It follows, therefore, that when we furnish the right conditions under which it is possible to know that we are a projection of God-not an image, not a reflection, but a projection of Spirit on the physical-plane-we can become open to receive the consciousness of the Divine. When we realize that this Light force of pure love resides within us, breathing through us, thinking through us, radiating from us, loving through us, we can begin to treasure the knowledge of our identity above all other knowledge.

When someone learns that a person nearly died and was whisked up into the Pearly Gates, there is a natural tendency to want to learn what that person saw and heard. People want to hear the stories of what near-death-experiencers saw and heard, because in my opinion, they are wondering if they too, or their loved ones who have died, will see and hear the same things when they die and enter the Pearly Gates.

Ever since Raymond Moody's book, *Life after Life* was published, there has been an explosion of books, articles, tapes, seminars, and lectures written on the subject of near-death experiences, as well as continuing research in the field. Learning about these experiences can be a great source of comfort to many people who wonder what life is like on the other side, or if life does in fact, exist following physical death.

As inspiring as beautiful scenes may be which have been described in many experiences, what I believe is the ultimate take-away from these experiences is the *message* coming from the voices of those who had transcendent otherworldly experiences. The message is not so much about what happens after we die, rather it is about the meaning of our existence and the nature of reality! It is more about *life* than it is about death!

That is what this book is about. I will offer the knowledge I was given by my Great Teacher, the Light-God, when I was invited into the Kingdom of Heaven. My glimpse into "Heaven" was not so much a *place* as it was a *condition* of the soul being released from the physical body and experiencing God as the ultimate reality. It was as if all eternity had opened up before me- a world that was familiar. I was "home" again with God. It is where I came from and where I will return after physical death. I call that "home" Heaven.

When Jesus was asked when the Kingdom of God would come, Jesus said it wasn't a place one would be able to see and point to. Instead, Jesus explained, "*Neither shall they say, Lo here! Or, lo there! For, behold, the kingdom of God is within you.*" (Luke 17:21) Heaven is indeed within, and is revealed by our *awareness*. That is the ultimate truth for all of us to realize, and the reason why I was given by Grace this message to share with humanity.

It is a message of discovery of what we ultimately are, the answer to the questions: Who am I? Why am I here?

Where am I going? What is life all about? The message I was sent back to share with others is about how we can shed our false impressions and false identity in order to tread the inner path toward full self-realization. **It's about using our time on earth to develop our spirituality and to know the reason for our being here.** It's about growing in awareness that human life is a wonderful opportunity to return to one's essential Oneness with the Divine. It's about learning to love and being so filled with love that we become aware that we are *in* the world but not *of* it. **It's about the realization of Divinity unfolding Itself as us.**

There is a natural tendency to be curious about what kind of person experiences unusual spiritual experiences and revelations. Are there some personality styles or characteristics or a particular lifestyle that predisposes someone to discover spiritual truths that originate from a Divine Source?

I freely acknowledge that I knew very little about religion, spirituality, metaphysics, philosophy, or mysticism when I received my invitation from God to enter into the Heavenly realm. I never had any formal religious education, and I had never read the Bible. I was an ordinary woman, wife, a mother, a career woman working as a cytology cancer researcher and cytology instructor at a major university and other laboratories until I retired and devoted my life to the spiritual work that I am so passionate about.

As an ordinary and simple woman, I am not competent to discuss the many different doctrinal differences between the many various religions. I am also aware that many people do not believe that God can appear to ordinary individuals like me, bringing messages for humanity as God once did during Biblical times. Yet, this is precisely what God did in my case! I would be less than faithful if I simply turned my back on this calling because I was afraid of what people would think of me. I could not turn my back on the Light-God who had specifically instructed me to pass this wisdom along to others.

My only intent is to share with others, the Divine reality I experienced with the conviction that what my Great Teacher revealed to me will help others to see a vision of life as a journey from total attachment to self to total attachment to the Divine and to the Divine way of life.

It is my hope that I will be able to inspire others to recognize the power of Spirit within, and to make the wholeness which already exists come forth, and manifest in form. It is with great joy and humility that I offer love from the Light, based on my journey into the Light. Together we can move forward into how life can be lived in the power of pure Divine Love. Together we can know there is an inner truth within the Self which yearns to be known, and that the expression of this truth makes a person whole in their own eyes as well as in the eyes of others.

At the heart of humanity, there is a deep yearning to know God, where our whole being is conscious of the Divine working in us. In our eagerness to learn more about the ultimate nature of life itself, we may call upon many sources to bring us those revelations so we may know them as truth. We may go from one spiritual teacher to another, or read books, or attend workshops, and still never get farther along the path to discovering our inner truth. We may get very discouraged and give up the quest for uncovering the mysteries of our Being.

I make an effort to stay true to the insights I've received from the Light, while at the same time being open to learning from the experiences (and research) of others. Stay connected to your own inner Source, but at the same time, learn from others.

Comparing notes with others helps us to gain clarity about all kinds of things that we are blind to on our own. For example, many of the pitfalls that we encounter on the spiritual path are the same for everyone. If we can talk about these challenges with others that are further along the path than we are, they can help us avoid them.

Even those with strong inner connections are deeply confused about all kinds of things. They really need help sorting things out, and that appears to be one of the main reasons that God gave us one another.

My Great Teacher, the Light-God, taught me that teachers, books and lectures are good up to a point, for they can talk *about* truth and lead people to the Divine. However, spiritual illumination can only come from our soul, or from our Divine Spirit within originating as a *direct experience.*

This sweet Presence unfolds its many gifts to us to the degree that we are open to receive them. The greater the degree of love we attain, the greater we allow our soul to express itself, its mission, and bring to our intellectual consciousness the awareness of the Divine within.

I have come to know that the Creator gave us two powerful abilities: to prove things we find hard to believe, and to believe in things we find hard to prove. I have also come to know that truth cannot be told; it must be *experienced.* Learning *about* truth is not the same as *knowing* truth. For when truth reveals itself, it is like a light bulb turning on, proclaiming from the deepest part of our being that we knew it all along, and we just remembered it. It's an a-ha moment! It rings true for us.

We can have all the intellectual knowledge that can fit into our computer-like brains and *know about* truth, but it's being *true* to what we know that concerns Spirit more about how we live our lives. The voice of our Great Teacher within automatically brings us a sense of peace whenever we do not compromise our integrity. That inner peace is knowing that our outer self matches our inner self.

To share the consciousness of the One who gifted me with this consciousness is, for me, one of life's greatest blessings. Because in sharing my story and my heart with others of the immense love our Creator has for **all of us** – with no exceptions – therein lies the seed that is planted, and the good will be done.

I am opening my heart and soul in this book, exposing the most intimate feelings I have. I realize that some people may label me crazy, or disbelieve that I was with the Light-God four times. But I accept that cynicism as part of my "calling." You see, during my experience I was given a life preview of what my life would be like should I accept this work on behalf of the Light. I was shown how people would ridicule and disbelieve me. I also saw how people would be inspired to lift their hearts closer to the Light because of my work.

I promised God that I would not renounce the gift I was given, but that I would do all I can to help bring others to the Light. This will be my small part going forward together, shoulder to shoulder, with our hearts beating as one and our minds flowing as one – for indeed we are one. My words one day will be forgotten, but perhaps if hearts are open to welcome the seed I scatter among those hearts the Spirit will awaken, letting God unfold and revealing to those hearts the Divine Love that I so freely speak of.

HEAVENLY MUSIC ORIGINATING FROM ONE MIND

Kitaro is a Grammy Award-winning Japanese New Age musician whose music, for me, evokes a spiritual flair that nurtures my Spirit in strangely mesmerizing ways. His music evokes a reflection of my deep inner self, the self that is one with the Light. So, in a sense, Kitaro's music gives a voice to all that is deep within me which is the very foundation of my being. It is a voice beyond words and beyond form from which crystal-pure Spirit readily flows within me. It is for this reason that, when I am writing my books, I listen to Kitaro's music playing softly in the background. The music tunes my body to receive a greater flow of creative ideas that I receive from Source as I write. Writing then becomes a holy, purposeful, and loving expression of my Higher Self that I can give to the world with love.

Kitaro's music is a reflection of the person he is and the philosophy he believes in. He was once interviewed in Down Beat and is reported telling John Diliberto:

"The sound has a power for humans, for nature. I took two speakers and in front of each I placed a flower. On one side came loud music, on the other side came my music. After one week, the flower in front of my music is bending towards the speaker, the other one is dead. I think it is the same thing for humans."

Now that I have introduced you to Kitaro and his music and why I want you to learn about this story and its relationship to my writing, I would like to tell you about a fascinating connection I had with Kitaro many years ago. One evening in the year 1986, I had a dream. In the dream, I had composed a beautiful, wordless song that was going to be introduced to the public during a concert performance.

The theater in which the concert was to be performed was filled to capacity. I walked down the aisle to my seat, anxiously awaiting that moment when the musicians would play the song I had composed. Soon the curtain opened and my song birthed into the musicians' instruments and filled the theater with the melodic sounds of all the notes I had composed in my mind. I was elated beyond words! The dream ended.

When I awoke the next morning, I retained the memory of that song and I began humming it all day long. For days, weeks, months, I couldn't get that beautiful song out of my mind. I felt that it was such a good song that perhaps one day, it would become a hit record. But I can't read or write music. I wasn't able to jot down the notes so I wouldn't forget that song, so I decided to hum the song into my tape recorder, thinking that perhaps one day, I could let a musician listen to it and the notes would then be transcribed and recorded. I put my tape-recorded song in a drawer and forgot about it.

One year later, I learned that Kitaro was going to perform at the Ohio Theater in Columbus, Ohio, where I lived at the time. Coincidentally, the performance was for one night and it happened to be on my birthday, September 23rd. My husband, knowing how much I love Kitaro's music, bought two tickets for us to attend the concert.

Thankfully, the old theater was beautifully refurbished by volunteers who had saved it from the wrecking ball, so when we walked down the aisle to go to our seats, I felt so enthused to witness what a beautiful theater Kitaro's performance was being held in.

The curtain was closed, awaiting that moment when the exciting concert performance would begin. A man's voice came over the loudspeaker.

"Ladies and gentlemen, we are pleased to announce that this evening's performance is Kitaro's first musical appearance in the United States. He will be playing songs from his new album, but please don't rush out to the stores to buy it yet, as the album has not yet been released. Wait a few more weeks so the stores can stock his album. Ladies and gentlemen, sit back and enjoy the show."

The curtain opened, and on stage were seven musicians. Kitaro was on synthesizers and two others were on keyboards, along with a guitarist, a violinist, a drummer, and a percussionist. Kitaro approached the microphone to address the audience. He apologized for not being able to speak the English language very well, but managed to convey that he was very happy to be in America for his first U.S.A. performance that evening. The audience applauded with enthusiasm and then it was time for his performance to begin.

How can I put into words what happened next? Perhaps by saying in just a few words that my dream one year earlier was being played out exactly how I had envisioned it.

Kitaro's musicians began playing the first song of the evening. It was MY song, the one I had composed in my dream a year earlier! *How can this be?* I wondered. Immediately, tears gushed from my eyes; my senses were being overloaded. My dream one year earlier was actually being played out in reality that evening. As you recall, in my dream I walked down the aisle of the theater, took my seat, and was very excited to listen to musicians playing the song I had composed! It was all unfolding for me in the physical reality that night.

My husband noticed how emotional I was and asked what was wrong. I couldn't tell him what was going on, so I just said that it was a great song being played and that I was enjoying it very much.

During the final song, Kitaro had a laser light beam projected over the audience, and it hovered over us during the entire song – MY song, the song in my dream. Kitaro began and ended his concert playing the song I had composed in my dream one year earlier. I watched the laser light sparkle and I sensed the presence of the Divine amidst all of us being expressed through this medium. Wherever we go, whatever we do, the Light is beside us and within us. It was a moment of pure joy and love! I left that concert performance that evening having added a new dimension to my understanding of alternate realities.

I have always wondered how and why this happened to me. I learned that Kitaro's Grammy Award Nominated album, "Kojiki," with that song, "Sozo," wasn't released until 1990. My dream occurred in 1986 and Kitaro's first performance was in the fall of 1987. There was no way I could have known he had written that song before I first heard it being played during his visit to America in 1987.

So the question is: Where did that song come from? I do not claim ownership to that song! It's Kitaro's song, or is it really? I found it interesting that Kitaro gives credit for his music to a power beyond him, as I do with my writing.

He is quoted during an interview with *Rolling Stone Magazine*,

"This music is not from my mind. It is from Heaven, going through my body and out my fingers through composing. Sometimes I wonder. I never practice. I don't read or write music, but my fingers move. I wonder, whose song is this? I write my songs, but they are not my songs."

For some reason unknown to me, for a moment, I was gifted with the ability to join the One Mind where all knowledge is present – that same reality I experienced during my near-death and near-death-like experiences, in that same place where time does not exist. It is my feeling, therefore, that Kitaro's music already exists in an alternate dimension, and is simply being "downloaded" to him when the time is right.

I can say the same thing about me when I write my books. I have always felt that I am not the true author, but rather, only the pencil in God's hand, recording the words that effortlessly flow through me. I say this because when the ego, "I," begins to write, I cannot write. But when I surrender my ego needs and raise my vibration through sincere prayer, love for God, and soft music playing, then the writing becomes inspired and flows through me easily. I honestly believe that my writing, as with Kitaro's music, comes from a Source independent from my physical brain. I believe it comes from a Higher Source. Knowing this personally, I can therefore understand why Kitaro also feels that his songs are not his, but come from Heaven as well.

As for me, this is just one story in the saga of my life; there have been many others as well. What I am consciously aware of is but a fraction of all that I am. I will always be grateful to the One who gifted me with the knowledge of my true identity as a Spirit being, vibrating on many levels like a chord of music in which many notes resonate together. I am also grateful that I am able to bear witness to the many ways the One True Light is actively lifting us to a spiritual peace through the gentle power of love, and that music is also a source of that great love.

2

FIRST THINGS FIRST

My Beloved,
Those who truly aspire to be instruments for Divine
Purpose will become guiding lights in the world to express
the connection between human and Divine Conscious-
ness.

NEAR-DEATH EXPERIENCES

There has been lots of information about near-death experiences ever since Raymond Moody, M.D. published his best-selling book, *Life After Life*. I was one of the many individuals who had a near-death experience in the early 1960's when Dr. Moody hadn't even performed his research yet. I died during complications of childbirth and woke up in the morgue! Obviously, I was extremely grateful when Dr. Moody's book appeared on the public scene, giving me and thousands of other experiencers the support that enabled us to know that we were not alone, and we were not crazy.

Years later, in 1979, while delivering a eulogy for a dear friend, I had another very profound experience every bit as detailed and life-transforming as a classic near-death

17

experience. However, at that time I was not close to death nor suffering serious illness or physical trauma. I will explain what happened to me in a few moments. But first I would like to refresh your memory of the features of a near-death experience so that you will be able to recognize the same features I experienced when I died, and also while I was delivering the eulogy.

With over forty-plus years of research that has taken place, we can now say that it is estimated that 15 million people in the U.S.A. have had a near-death experience, or NDE according to a Gallop Poll in 1997. It is estimated that between 15% and 18% of all people who face a life-threatening event will experience a near-death experience. Similar statistics are coming in from around the world. With children, it's estimated that 85% who experienced cardiac arrest have had a NDE. (Source: International Association for Near-Death Studies, Inc. and noted researcher PMH Atwater, who studied over 270 child cases.)

Atwater has found that the "typical" NDE doesn't hold up in broad-based studies. It is misleading to assume that all experiencers leave their bodies, go through a tunnel into the light, meet deceased relatives in Heaven, and are then told to come back. Noted NDE researcher Jeffrey Long, M.D. and his wife, Jody, hosts the world's largest NDE website www.nderf.org. They have accumulated valuable information from 613 NDErs who participated in their online questionnaires. Dr. Long published his findings in his New York Times best-selling book, *Evidence of the Afterlife: The Science of Near-Death Experiences*. He lists the main elements of a near-death experience and what percentage of those 613 individuals recalled experiencing each element.

1. Out-of-body experience (OBE) 75.4%
2. Heightened senses 74.4%

3. Intense and generally positive emotions or feelings 76.2%

4. Passing into or through a tunnel 33.8%

5. Encountering a mystical or brilliant light 66.6%

6. Encountering other beings, either mystical beings or deceased relatives or friends 57.3%

7. A sense of alteration of time and space 60.5%

8. Life review 22.2%

9. Encountering unworldly ("heavenly") realms 40.6%

10. Encountering or learning special knowledge 56% (31.5% answered that they felt they understood everything about the universe," 31.3% felt they understood everything "about myself and others.")

11. Encountering a boundary or barrier 31%

12. Return to the body, either voluntary or involuntary 58.5%

According to the research, there are many individuals who had a hellish or frightening NDE with feelings of extreme fear, isolation, non-being, confusion, occasional torment, or guilt.

Two studies have reported the percentage of these NDEs as 17% and 18% (Rommer, 2006), and (Bush,2006.) Two online NDE sites report incidences of 8.6% and 15%, (Migliore, 2007), and Long, http://www.nderf.org.)

These individuals were often ordinary, "good" people. This is contrary to what many people and fundamentalists believe, that only murderers, rapists, and vile people wind up in hell. There is no evidence that links hellish experiences with "bad" people.

I would recommend a book written by Nancy Evans Bush called *Dancing Past the Dark*. She is herself an experiencer of a distressing NDE and has researched the subject of distressing NDEs. Her book is the first comprehensive look at these experiences, and is an effective guide to understanding, living with, and learning from them.

Let's learn now how near-death experiences affect the individuals having them. Generally speaking, approximately 85% of individuals having this experience have been changed for life. Research has reported shifts in personality, attitudes, and behavior with the following psychological features:

- Loss of the fear of death
- Increased self-esteem
- Increased concern for others
- Reduced desire for materialistic gains
- Hunger for knowledge
- Greater appreciation for nature
- Latent abilities surface
- Increased belief in an afterlife
- Greater sense of inner peace even while facing difficulties in life
- Reduced suicidal tendencies
- More spiritual, less religious
- Increased compassion for others
- Become more loving and forgiving of others
- Less competitive
- Convinced of a life purpose
- Increase in intuitive and psychic abilities
- Able to live more in the present moment than in the past or future
- Many change careers to be able to work in a career that will help others in some way – a business executive may return to school to become a nurse, a teacher, a social worker, a psychologist, etc.

The following are some of the physiological changes:
- More sensitive to pharmaceuticals
- More intelligent
- Sensitivity to light and sound
- Physically younger looking
- Healing abilities
- Electrical sensitivities – a condition whereby the energy surrounding the experiencer affects nearby electrical equipment and technological devices.

  Examples include: watches stop working, TV channels change by themselves, light bulbs pop, problems with computers suddenly losing power or doing weird things, and so on

EXPERIENCES THAT MIMIC A NEAR-DEATH EXPERIENCE

There are many names for experiences that share common features of a near-death experience. They include: *near-death-like (NDLE), out-of-body (OBE), visions, exceptional human experience, (EHE), spiritually transformative experience (STE), nearing death awareness (NDA), shared NDE, peak experience, religious experience, mystical experience, revelation experience, unitive experience, and probably more.* Actually, they all belong to the *family* of mystical experiences. It is no wonder that there is confusion when discussing them.

For now, I am going to talk about the near-death-like and spiritually transformative experience because they really are one in the same. This was my most intense and life-transforming experience. As you read about it shortly, you will soon see the similarities to the classic NDE that I have just described. I experienced all 12 of the components that Dr. Long cited in his study, with the exception of encountering a boundary or barrier. I also experienced an additional component not mentioned: a life preview.

Experiences very similar to near-death experiences happen to many people. In 2004, the National Opinion Research Center at the University of Chicago found that 50% of Americans polled have had a spiritual or religious experience that changed their lives.

In 1992 the International Association for Near-Death Studies, Inc. (IANDS), sent out a questionnaire asking their members how they came to their NDEs. Of those who responded, 229 were experiencers. Among this group, 23% said their experience occurred during clinical death, 40% during serious illness or physical trauma, and 37% percent without those events happening. More recently, IANDS conducted another survey of 800 people who submitted their experience to the IANDS online NDE archives, and found that one-fourth of the 800 people claimed not to be close to death at the time. Rather, they were involved in doing ordinary activities such as praying, meditating, or in some kind of stressful situation at the time.

I conducted my own study of 102 individuals who were not close to death nor suffering serious illness or physical trauma, and published my findings in my book, *Divine Moments: Ordinary People Having Spiritually Transformative Experiences*, 2012. I found the same features and aftereffects in these individuals as I found being reported in near-death experiences.

Some of the situations that triggered the experiences in my study included: being at rest, being at work, being at play, praying, meditating, driving a car, dreaming, watching television, flying an airplane, and talking on the phone.

Bottom line: Coming close to death is only one trigger for

this type of transcendent otherworldly spiritual experience. There are many triggers, and each one should be considered no more or less important than the other, because these spiritual experiences are bringing back, from the mouths of the individuals having them, the same message – LOVE one another!

I strongly encourage the researchers of near-death experiences to engage in more near-death-like studies. So much valuable information is being lost by refusing to include these experiences in the studies. I can't tell you how many times I was refused permission to participate in NDE studies because I had a near-death-like experience. *"Your experience doesn't count,"* or, *"We're only studying near-death experiences right now,"* was the familiar voice of the researchers. Of course near-death-like experiences count! There are probably thousands if not millions of other individuals who had experiences very similar to a near-death experience who were not close to death at the time. Why close the door to all those individuals who have something of importance to share with humanity? Why not broaden our understanding of transcendence, the Light, the Love, and the transformations that are similarly happening to most people having these same experiences?

I've spent decades voicing my opinion on this important matter, and one day I hope that my pioneering efforts will pay off for the many experiencers who are being excluded by the NDE research studies today. To be fair, there is some work being done in this area. Some authors have included accounts of near-death-like experiences in their books, and some researchers have acknowledged the fact that coming close to death is only one trigger. A few small studies have been done, and a few prominent NDE websites are beginning to include these accounts online. However, as a strong advocate for near-death-like experiences, more research needs to be done in this area of investigation.

Do you recall that in the days before Moody published his book, *Life after Life*, NDErs were afraid to talk about their near-death experiences? Only after more information became available to the general public through research, books, and other media did it become safe for experiencers to talk about their experiences. Look how much information we have gleaned from these experiences, after 40 years of scientific studies. Well, I know that there are many individuals who are afraid to speak about their near-death-like experiences for the same reason early NDErs were afraid to speak of their experiences. Until we can support all who have had transcendent experiences, we will miss out on what they have to teach us.

3

FOUR TIMES WITH THE LIGHT–GOD

My Beloved,
I will lead you in a Spirit-led direction into a deeper
fellowship with Me, deeper than you could ever have
imagined. I want you to know Me, not just know about
Me. Take My Hand and I will lead you into My Light.

MY CHILDHOOD VISIT WITH GOD

There are many ways people learn about our Creator, e.g. religious scholars, clergy, churches, synagogues, universities, books, movies, etc. I had no formal training about our Creator, but I would like to tell you how I came to *know* our Creator rather than knowing *about* our Beloved. It is my hope that as you turn each page in this book you will clearly see that our Creator has the absolute authority to open our eyes, and hearts to a more profound understanding of our Beloved's Divine nature, no matter who that person is, how young, how old, how educated, how uneducated, or what religion a person had or did not have. I would like to tell you how I first met my Beloved.

My early childhood roots played an important role in preparing me to receive the gift of my Holy Heavenly encounter with the Light in my later adult years. I recall as a small child having had a wee mystical experience that activated my spiritual relationship with our Creator and set into motion the deep reverent love I have felt for my Beloved for the rest of my life.

I am a Ukrainian Catholic. My grandparents fled Ukraine during the Russian Revolution and managed to settle in a coal-mining town in Hazleton, Pennsylvania. The language spoken in our home was mainly English laced with Ukrainian so that everyone could understand one another. My grandparents spoke very little English. Simple words were spoken which reflected the non-intellectual life we all led.

I was born in 1941 and times back then were very hard. World War II began, and men were needed to fight the war. My father joined the navy and was sent to the Philippines as a Seabee, constructing runways for our warplanes to land on. While my dad was away at war, mother and we three children lived with grandma and grandpa. My childhood days were filled with laughter, love, and joyful moments spent with grandma baking bread and the best poppy seed rolls imaginable. We were poor, but I never knew it. I felt deeply loved and secure.

The earliest memory I have is of a three or four-year old little girl sitting on a church pew, her tiny legs just barely dangling over the edge of the wooden oak pew. My mother always made me sit to her left and my two brothers to her right.

"*Sit still; be quiet, don't turn around to look at people,*" mother would say.

"*We are in God's house now and you must be very good children.*"

God's house? I wondered. Who is God? What does God look like? I don't see Him, I thought. Then mother explained to me that God lives far away up in Heaven, up past the sky. The church was a place where God's Spirit lives, and it is a very Holy place where people come to visit Him. I didn't understand what God's "Spirit" was, but my mother answered my questions, and that's all I needed to know at that time.

Going to church every Sunday was BORING! We went to High Mass (the longer of the two masses-almost two hours long!) Not only did I have to sit still and not fidget for two hours, but I also couldn't understand a word the priest said. He spoke entirely in Ukrainian, because most of the people who belonged to the church were Ukrainian immigrants. I could understand the language in our home because we spoke simple sentences; *"Close the door, wipe your feet, supper is ready,"* and so on. The priest was speaking words I had never heard in our home. His words reflected a superior degree of intellectualism about a subject that I knew nothing about.

Seated in the pew, I just stared at the priest watching his every move. I couldn't understand why a man would want to dress up in something called a "robe." It looked like a woman's long dress to me. A very long necklace hung from his neck and fell to his waist where a tasseled ropelike belt hugged his thick waist. Mother explained to me that the necklace he was wearing was the "symbol of the cross." Draped over his hands was something that looked like a bracelet with pretty colored beads. Once again, mother explained that it was the "rosary."

I couldn't understand anything mother was trying to teach me about this odd-looking man who talked in a weird language. To confuse me more, at times this man that mother called the "priest" walked around the altar whirling a gold pot hanging from a long golden chain. Smoke was gushing out from the top of the pot. As he stood in front of the people sitting in the pews, he whirled the pot as high as his shoulders so that the smoke would reach everyone. I always coughed when the smoke touched my nose, and I asked mother why he was doing this. She told me that he was "blessing everyone."

Nothing made any sense to me, and I hated coming to this place every Sunday. It was an ordeal for my brothers and me to follow the rules of etiquette to which our mother made us adhere. But we knew that if we didn't follow them, our little behinds would get tanned when we got home. Disobedience was not an option. We obeyed Mother's rules.

Seated like a rigid statue in the church pew, I decided that I had to do something to occupy myself during the two-hour church service. I thought, "*Since this is where God lives, I'll talk to Him silently,*" since I wasn't allowed to speak aloud. I can still remember that day as if it were yesterday. Silently in my mind, I started talking to God, explaining why I couldn't talk out loud. Wondering if God could hear my silent words, I continued to talk about my family, and the activities that I did all week. I told God about the pierogis that grandma and I made for supper Friday night and asked God if He had ever tasted them.

"*They're delicious,*" I said. "*First you make a dough out of flour, water and stuff. You roll it out thin, cut them in squares, then put a spoonful of mashed potatoes on the dough and then you fold the dough over the potatoes and pinch the edges closed with your fingers.*" I said. "*Then grandma puts the pierogis in boiling water, and I have to tell her when they float to the top. Here's the best part God, Grandma takes them out of the pot and puts them on my plate with lots of melted butter, fried*" *onions and sour cream. I can eat a lot of pierogis God; they are delicious!"* I said in quiet conversation with God in my mind.

I talked to God as if I were talking to my mother. Words kept flowing effortlessly. My eyes were open, but my intense focus on my silent conversation with God obliterated all my surroundings so that all I saw was a misty, fog-like presence before me. I no longer saw the priest, the altar, the altar boys, and the stained-glass windows. Deep in a meditative-like state, I was able to transcend unknowingly, to a place where I felt so safe and loved and where I was nestled close to my friend, God.

I remember saying in my thoughts, "I have to go now God, but I love you very much. Thanks for listening to me."

Then clearly and unmistakable, I heard a masculine voice in my head saying, *"I love you also my child!"*

My mother's elbow beside me disrupted my prayerful state and I soon returned to full awareness of my surroundings. It was time to leave. Mass was over.

I never told mother about my silent conversation with God that day, but from that day on, I couldn't wait to go to church on Sundays. All week I would collect and save all the thoughts I wanted to share with God during the service on Sunday. I was easily able to transcend my physical boundaries and enter that wondrous place where my friend God was, simply by praying. I never heard God's Voice again as I did that first time, but I knew that our Creator was always close beside me, closer than my mother sitting next to me. I felt a loving bond with my Beloved that was **REAL** and not a figment of my young imagination.

MY SECOND VISIT WITH GOD DURING A NEAR-DEATH EXPERIENCE

The year was 1962, and I died during childbirth, the result of eclampsia of pregnancy. My blood pressure had sky-rocketed; I had severe edema, and convulsions, resulting in my death. The instant I died, my spirit-self lifted from my physical body and floated to the ceiling, where I was able to observe the commotion taking place below. I saw my motionless physical body and I felt completely detached from it. It was as if I was looking at a coat that I no longer needed. I had no use for that physical body anymore. The body was simply the garment that I wore that housed my real self – my soul. But now my soul had been set free from the constraints of that physical body. I felt more *alive* and ecstatic than at any other time in my physical life. I could still see and hear everything while continuing to be full of life, although in a different form.

How does one explain the ineffable to one who has never experienced this phenomenon? Words are limiting. They can't convey the magnitude of experiencing something that is beyond our known physical senses. So I will try to do the best I can with the limited language we have been given, knowing that this is probably a futile attempt to communicate the ineffable.

Darkness as deep as the deepest night enveloped my soul the moment I died and lifted out of my physical body. The dark void was a place that welcomed me as if the entire universe had awaited my arrival. Extreme bliss and unearthly peace were the emotions I felt as the darkness penetrated my soul. The dark void nurtured me with a safe and protective power so that fear was non-existent. Nothing on earth could compare with the tremendous bliss that I was feeling!

Meanwhile, I would occasionally look down below at the medical staff trying to revive my dead body. There were a lot of frenzied doctors and nurses that I could see, and I wondered why they were fussing so much over my physical body. It didn't make sense to me. Couldn't they just look up towards the ceiling and see me? Then they would know I was still alive, albeit without that physical body. I didn't need that physical shell disguising my real self anymore. So why were they trying to revive me and spoil my beautiful and blissful new life that I was experiencing outside of that physical body they were working on? I couldn't understand it.

A nurse was pounding on my chest yelling,

"*Come back, Nancy, come back!*"

I didn't want to come back! A brilliant Light was approaching me and when I saw it, I *knew* I was in the presence of God! The only thing I wanted, was to go to the Light; nothing else mattered. Tender, sweet love was radiating from the Light-God and I wanted to embrace every bit of it that my soul could contain.

But the nurse kept pounding on my chest yelling,

"*Come back Nancy, come back! You have a son, come back!*"

I knew my new-born son would be alright. That feeling was imparted into my awareness of everything that was happening. I just knew I didn't have to worry about him.

I was tired of being pulled in two different directions – to make a decision to return to physical consciousness or to continue my journey with the Light-God. I just wanted that nurse to stop her incessant nagging for me to come back, and by deciding to do what she was telling me, I felt that would put an end to her annoying yelling. I woke up in the morgue!

To this day I can still feel the cold metal gurney my body

was lying on in the morgue and feeling a sheet covering my entire body from my toes to the top of my head. With my fingers, I took the sheet that covered my face and pulled it down to my chest. I heard noises in the room as if someone else was there, but since I was lying on my back face-up toward the ceiling, I didn't see anything except the ceiling lights. I remember turning my head to my right side and seeing another metal gurney with a body lying on it with a sheet covering it just as I was. I turned my head back toward the center of my body and that's when I blacked out. The next awareness I had was waking up in a hospital room, confused by all that had happened to me.

Remember, this was in the early 1960's. There was no information about what I experienced, so for fear of being labeled crazy and being transferred off the maternity ward onto the psych ward, I was not going to tell anyone what I saw and heard.

However, when my physician came to talk to me, I was very anxious to talk with him to find out what happened. I immediately asked him,

"*What happened to me, what went wrong?*"

He looked as if he saw a ghost. I could see that he was very uncomfortable. He said,

"*Nothing went wrong, nothing.*"

I replied with a rather convincing tone in my voice,

"*Yes, something did go wrong and I want to know.*"

He just kept trying to change the subject but I stood my ground.

"*It's my right to know what happened doctor, so please tell me,*" I said.

Finally, he put his arm around my shoulder and said,

"*Look, I'm an excellent physician. Trust me. You want to have more children, don't you?*"

Well, to be honest, that was the last thing on my mind at that time, so I just casually told him yes. But I really didn't like the thought of having to go through another 39 brutal hours of labor without any medication and die in the process. I figured if I just said yes, we didn't need to talk about that part anymore. I wanted to get straight to the subject of what happened to me that he didn't want to talk about.

"*Mrs. Clark,*" he said, "*I'm afraid if I told you what happened, it will do a lot of psychological damage and you will never, ever want to have children again. So put this out of your mind. From this day forward, don't look back. Forget what happened and move ahead with your life.*"

I persisted in trying to get him to tell me what went wrong, but he would not discuss it with me any further. He left the room quickly, probably so he wouldn't have to answer any more of my questions.

Since I had been absolutely committed to secrecy concerning what happened to me so that I wouldn't be committed to a mental health facility, I decided to do just as the physician suggested. I moved on with my life, never sharing with anyone my near-death experience.

After I had recovered well enough, the nurse brought my son to me and placed him in my arms. To this day, I can still remember that moment as vividly as I remember being with the Light–God when I died. My son looked into my eyes and I knew at that moment that God had given me one of His finest little angels in Heaven for me to love and take care of. No longer did I agonize the separation between the Light–God and me, nor did I regret the decision I made to return back to life again. My newborn son needed me, and yes, I needed him as well.

Even though my son is a grown man, I continue to tell

him the story of when he was placed in my arms after his birth, and I continue to sing him the song that he so often heard me singing to him as a young boy. It is a song from the 1950's called, "*You Are My Special Angel*," recorded by the Vogues. The lyrics in part go like this. "*You are my special angel, sent from up above. The Lord smiled down on me and sent an angel to love*," etc.

I am very grateful that the nurse who kept hitting my chest and yelling at me to "come back" kept irritating me to the point where I finally gave in and came back to life again. I'm sure she will witness what happened during her life review knowing that she pestered me until I made the decision to come back. I'm sure that her life-review scene will bring a smile to her soul. Thank you, dear nurse; I love you.

Near-death experiences were not being reported during those early 1960's. Raymond Moody had not yet published his best-selling book, *Life after Life*. Did I dare tell anyone what I saw and heard while my soul had exited my physical body when I died? Who would believe me? I became fearful that if I spoke to anyone about this, I would be considered mentally unstable. The best thing for me to do was to remain silent and never speak a word about this to anyone. I knew the reality of my near-death experience, and I simply tucked it away in the far recesses of my memory, that is, until God came looking for me again years later in 1979, and invited me to Heaven's door once more. This time I didn't have to die, come close to death, or suffer serious illness or physical trauma.

MY THIRD VISIT WITH GOD DURING MY NEAR-DEATH-LIKE EXPERIENCE

In recent years, researchers have acknowledged that there are experiences very similar to classic near-death experiences, so they have termed these similar experiences, *near-death-like experiences*. Near-death-like experiences have the same components of a near-death experience with the exception that the individual was not close to death nor suffering serious illness or physical trauma.

It isn't about the events leading up to the otherworldly transcendent experience that matters, it is the **experience itself that is important!** The experience *begins* the moment consciousness lifts out of the physical body and enters into a dimension or reality other than the physical realm. That's the experience! Sure, the physical events such as a car crash, heart attack, etc. leading up to the transcendent experience are interesting to learn about, but those events are **not the experience itself.** They are merely the *triggers* that precede the actual transcendent experience. And there are many triggers for this type of experience; coming close to death is but one trigger.

The resulting confusion about these terms has caused many individuals, who were not close to death at the time of their experience, to shy away from talking about it. Many of these individuals told me they don't feel as if their experiences are being validated by others, feeling that the only ones who are perceived as being credible are the ones who came close to death.

I suppose this is understandable, because to date we have had forty-plus years of scientific research in the field of near-death experiences. There are lots of accounts from individuals who were under anesthesia during surgery for example, who upon recovering described what the surgeon was talking about during the operation and described in detail the instruments that the surgeon used. There could be no way of knowing this unless the patient was indeed, out-of-body and actually viewing the scene below. As a result, it is hard to dismiss near-death experiences as hallucinations, wish fulfillment, or anything other than what they really are – very real experiences. It isn't so easy to verify someone's transcendent experience when they were praying, sitting quietly in a chair, or watching television, even though they may have experienced the same otherworldly events as someone who came close to death.

It is my feeling that these near-death-like experiences unfold in the same way by initiating a process of spiritual transformation within the individual in the same way that those who came close to death. They, like near-death experiencers, have received revelatory spiritual insights to be shared with humanity. In any event, the implications for all transcendent type of experiences is important for us to consider because I believe they reveal to us and point us in the direction of awakening to the higher meanings of human existence. I also believe that our Creator is enabling ordinary people to bring messages of love and hope to humanity in this day and age, perhaps when we need it the most in our history of civilization. It is important that we listen and learn from the many individuals who were gifted by God's Grace to bring back the messages from the other side, no matter how one got there in the first place.

Okay, now that I have given you some background information on what constitutes a near-death and similar near-death-like experience, I will describe the near-death-like experience I had in the winter of 1979, which forever transformed my life.

Simply put, God came looking for me during a time when I was completely conscious and perfectly healthy, both mentally and physically. I was not taking drugs of any kind. I was delivering a eulogy at the time. I still had not yet learned of Ray Moody, his book, or anything about near-death experiences.

As I began delivering the eulogy, I felt an unearthly peace filling my physical body. My deceased friend, whose eulogy I was delivering, held my right hand. I can only describe his presence with me as experiencing him through some super-natural manner, as I did not see him with my physical eyes. I knew he was with me and he was reassuring me that he was very happy. Then, powerfully yet with extreme gentle-ness, my soul lifted out of my physical body and merged into complete union with the Light-God.

Every fiber of my soul was lit aflame with the Light. Bright was my vision, so bright that a trillion suns all fused together would not replicate the intense brilliance emanating from the Light directly into my soul. I had no physical material eyes to see this brilliance. If I had, I certainly would have been blinded by the Light. My sight was not of this earthly realm.

A surge of energizing unconditional love poured from the Light-God into my consciousness. An indescribable euphoria that extended beyond human comprehension had intermingled with the Light's blissful Love as I was being welcomed "home." Words are silent and non-existent to describe my feelings at this point. So I will pause for a moment, as I remain silent with my own thoughts, to remember that Divine Love, a Love that still wells up within my physical body, even though so many years have passed.

I did nothing on my own to initiate this Sacred encounter with our Creator. It was my soul that the Creator so lovingly lifted from my physical body and led me to our Heavenly "home" all the while my physical body was delivering the eulogy for a dear friend who had died. I felt no resistance on my part as my soul was being whisked up and transformed into Divine Sacred Light.

A great moment of beauty touched my soul as I began to be filled with God's Light and unconditional Love. The radiance increased, transforming me from ordinary waking consciousness into Divine Consciousness.

The truth of my being was revealed to me as I began to awaken to the inner knowledge long buried within. It was as if I were being re-born with new eyes to see through, and new ears to hear what was being revealed to me by God. I completely merged into Oneness with the Light-God, seeing and understanding all things through the Creator's consciousness with no need to question or doubt anything. Truth was self-evident. Something *beyond* the known, the mystery of the unknown had revealed itself to me in that moment of Oneness with the Light-God.

No longer was I a separate self; the illusion of my separate "self" had melted away so that I lived in God and God lived in me. Earthly language is nonexistent to describe the joy, ecstasy, and rapture that embodied my being as God drew me into Himself.

My soul's trajectory into the Being of Light, in which the highest form of love was encountered, was the feeling of ecstasy, as my entire being was consumed with the very Presence of the Creator. I had no delusions about what I was experiencing. All my previous beliefs and convictions were seemingly being erased as I stood before the Creator in all my innocence.

A pure Spirit, my consciousness was elevated to know the Divine nature of myself. The luminous quality of the radiance within was so overwhelmingly beautiful to me! Wonderful concepts of truth were being fed into my mind from a heightened spiritual splendor, winging their way to me with lucid wisdom, and revealing to me all that I had forgotten while my soul had been inhabiting a physical body on earth. I was "home" again with the Source of all that Is or ever will be. I call that Source, God.

You will note throughout the book that I refer to God in the masculine gender. I do this only because I want to convey more of a personal, intimate "Being" rather than an impersonal Light. Actually, I did not experience the Light as being masculine or feminine. I experienced the Light as energy, as Love. If you are uncomfortable with me using the masculine word "He or His," please substitute the word you feel more comfortable using. After all, language is a barrier in this respect, and we are really talking about the same thing anyway.

I was remembering truths, revelations of wonderful intensity, convictions which cannot be reasoned out of existence. My God-given lucidity struck deep into my soul, healing the wounds of my past, as the exquisite splendor, beauty, and peace of Divinity shone forth from the Light. My ego had dissolved into intense, infinite love and it was overwhelming! In that state of non-ego, I was united into Oneness with the Light-God, experiencing the closeness and the supreme gift of Light consciousness- the Eternal state of Being.

I now understand that I needed the consciousness of the Light and the Light's Love as a basis for understanding the teachings I would be given so that the Light's message to the world would be pure.

The Light and I traveled through the dark universe at a tremendous rate of speed. I observed around 11 dimensions or realms as I was being transported to the beginning of creation. I understood that everything created has, at its core, the Light!

All communication was telepathic. There was no time; everything that was happening was occurring at the same "time," or simultaneously.

At one point, I had a life review. I was judging my own earthly life as I witnessed every moment of it with great clarity. Truth was now my awareness as I saw the times when I made bad choices by placing masks over my human perceptions of fear and ego-consciousness. All the while, the Light was still loving me unconditionally and not judging me for the mistakes I made. With new understanding about the meaning of life and our purpose, I resolved to be a better person upon my return to the earth plane.

During my near-death-like experience, I wanted to stay with the Light forever. So great was my desire to stay with the Light that I knew my soul had to be permanently separated from my physical body, so I contemplated giving my physical body a heart attack. Very quickly, the Light interrupted my thoughts and said to me,

"No, you cannot stay. I have work for you on earth. You are to become a communicator, to help people to understand there is life after death. Help them to become aware of their true nature, and help them to learn to live their lives expressing unconditional love for one another."

When I confirmed my promise to fulfill this calling, I was given a life preview in which I was shown both the negative and positive aspects of the work I was being called to do. I accepted with great love what the Light-God was asking of me. Once I promised to serve in this way, total knowledge was 'downloaded' into my consciousness. However, I was not permitted to recall everything, only certain parts. That doesn't mean I don't have all the answers. I do, but they are repressed for whatever reason. I was not permitted to bring back all the knowledge I received.

However, when I write with God or sometimes at odd times, the wisdom surfaces. It's as if God is "allowing" me to bring certain information to the forefront of my consciousness when the time is right for whatever reason.

After all knowledge was downloaded into my consciousness, I had a vision of sitting at the head of a large wooden table along with twelve individuals who were dressed in what appeared to be monk's clothes. They wore brown hooded robes which were tied with a rope-like belt at the waist. They wore sandals on their feet.

All but three individuals had their faces covered with their hoods so I couldn't see who they were. Even though the three men seated to my right had their faces revealed, I did not know who they were. They were complete strangers. I understood that the purpose of that meeting with the twelve individuals was to let me know that they were going to be part of my "mission" when I returned to the earthly realm. They each promised to help me fulfill my destiny.

A few years after my experience, I met those three men who were seated at the large wooden table with me whose faces were not covered with their robed hoods. They each lived in different states. I was shocked when I met them because I instantly recognized them from my experience. I never met them previously during my earthly life, so you can imagine the surprise I felt when that part of my experience was confirmed in the physical reality. How can I explain how this can happen?

There is no time on the other side. Everything can happen simultaneously and the soul can see into the past or the future. A soul living in the physical reality can also look past the veil and into the other world of spirit simultaneously, just as I did during my near-death-like experience. It is my understanding that the twelve individuals in my experience had this type of experience but were not allowed to recall it in their physical consciousness, just as I was not permitted to recall everything that I experienced. This would allow those individuals to carry out their part in my "mission" without their human egos interfering, thus preventing them from fulfilling their part in my spiritual work. I am puzzled, however, as to why they were all dressed in monk's apparel and the scene seemed to indicate an ancient time period.

I did not tell those individuals that I "met" them previously during my near-death-like experience, or that they had promised to help me with my calling. If I told them, I did not want them to feel any responsibility to help me. I knew that their souls knew what they were meant to do, and I would leave it up to their souls to manifest whatever help they were voluntarily willing to offer me. They did help me enormously, and because of the gratitude I had for them, I decided to tell them of my experience and their role in it after many years had passed so that I could thank them. Each person told me they sensed a deep desire within to help me, to support me, guide me, and lead me. As I said before, their souls knew what they were meant to do, and intuitively, their hearts were led to offer the kind of help I needed to further my work for the Light-God. Each person surrounded me with their Light of love and joy, and I experienced it radiating from them as sunbeams radiate from the sun. My gratitude and love for them is eternal.

What about the other nine individuals? Have they appeared in my life as well? As I said, during my experience, everyone had their hoods covering their faces except three, so I did not see who they were. There have been individuals who have appeared in my life to assist me in very big ways, and I have a hunch that they are some of those nine unidentified individuals seated at the wooden table in my experience. I, too, am grateful for the love and help they have given me!

At the center of every human being is the One whose love for us is so great that it flows through others to others. It becomes a blending of loving consciousness that, when recognized, goes into deeper levels of our being so that we can know with certainty that this love will bring to us what God has intended for us to perceive. Love will open closed doors, and by golly, the twelve individuals who are helping me without recognition have, and I'm sure will continue to, open more doors for me with the help of the Light that is within each of them.

I have never revealed their names and I intend to honor their privacy. But each person knows how grateful I am for their help. God bless them!

As my experience was approaching the end, the Light began to separate from me and fade into the distance, becoming dimmer. My heart was breaking! I didn't want the Light to go. But I knew that this would only be temporary, because one day, when I die, I would return once more to the Light. I knew I would be able to wait for that day. Placed deep in my heart, the Light said one word: "Book." As if my entire soul/body had opened up to receive that one word, I understood that God wanted me to remember to write and to convey to the masses all that He had asked me to do upon my return back to the earth plane. With that one word, I was given by Grace, the passion to do what was being asked of me.

I rapidly returned to my physical body as I was finishing up delivering the eulogy. From then on, my life would never be the same.

Incidentally, I should point out that receiving total knowledge from the Light is what many other near-death experiencers also report following their experiences. It seems that we each have been given different pieces of the puzzle, but not the entire puzzle. Only God has that complete one. Beware of anyone claiming to have remembered total knowledge, for that should raise a red flag for you! The research just does not support this claim. Just as there are flawed people in every profession, there are also flawed people in the spiritual vocation as well, who are not honest and who exaggerate their experiences. Be careful of who you can trust.

The communications presented to my consciousness were not the result of my own mental processes; I admit they were the work of an intellect far superior to my own. How, then, am I to try to convince anyone why one has such an inward conviction? Those who have also experienced the Light during their near-death experiences and others who have had mystical experiences will need no proof. Those who have doubts as to the source of my knowledge will only understand when they themselves have had similar experiences, or when they cross over the veil at the end of their lives. Those on the spiritual path who are drawn to learn about specific knowledge that is supportive of the evolution of their higher self will draw whatever meaning that will honor their own personal truths.

MY FOURTH VISIT WITH THE LIGHT-GOD

I have only shared this particular experience with a few friends, but I think I should speak publicly about it at this time. Once again, the memory of it stands out in my mind as if it happened yesterday. It was during the early 1980's when the Light-God appeared to me again. I had been up late that evening watching television. It was around 1:30 am and I was getting ready for bed. The electric blanket was warming up the bed nicely for me while I was putting on my pajamas. My husband was sound asleep so I undressed quietly so as not to disturb him. Outside I could hear the wind howling through the frigid January temperature. I was glad I had turned on that electric blanket. Just the thought of what it was like outdoors made me shiver. Fresh snow had been falling all night with an accumulation of about 2 inches on the ground, and it was still snowing.

Before I climbed into bed, I suddenly heard these words that appeared in my mind. *"Go outside Nancy and wait for me."*

I had no idea what was happening. Where did those words come from?

Are you crazy Nancy, I thought? *It's freezing outside! No, you're not going anywhere except into that nice warm bed!*

I wondered why I had even thought of doing something as insane as that. I quickly disregarded the thought and turned my attention to climbing into that nice warm bed that was awaiting me.

Again, those words were repeated in my mind. Only this time, I began to feel differently. Something deep within me – a feeling, – a knowing, that this was something that I truly needed to do. I felt an inflowing of peace and assurance compelling me to trust that what was happening was going to be okay.

Understanding what my Great Teacher taught me during my experience about the role of ego and soul, I knew that I had entered into a state of communion with my higher Self, enabling me to be in a state of receptivity. The mind cannot fathom that which it has never recognized. I had come to know since my experience that the voice of my inner Divine Spirit had made itself known to my physical body in such a way, leaving me to comprehend a revelation of wonderful intensity, a conviction which cannot be reasoned out of existence.

There was a sense of urgency with those words I heard in my mind, an urgency that immediately led me scurrying outside without putting on my winter coat, boots, gloves or scarf. Pajamas and my bedroom slippers were all I wore, yet once outside, I never felt cold. Odd.

I walked part way into the woods and looked up into the sky as snowflakes fell onto my face, with the cold wind blowing through my hair. The moon was missing from my sight, being obscured by the dark, thick snow clouds in my line of vision. Suddenly, the Light appeared to me. I recognized the Light. Of course I did! It was the Light-God! My consciousness was illumined to know the truth of what I was experiencing. This was no hallucination!

Having transcended the five senses, my intuitive faculty was alert, receptive, and responsive to the things of the Spirit. I felt the actual presence of God. Such beautiful peace and love flowed through my inner being as I gazed upon the brilliance of the Light. The Light communicated the following words to me.

"Nancy, there is a time coming when there will be a clash between positive and negative energy on the planet. It is a time when all beings must radiate as much positive (loving) energy out into the world. Whichever energy (positive or negative) is the most powerful, will decide man's fate. Do this while there is still time."

The Light disappeared and I was left still standing with my eyes focused upwards toward the sky. Humbled by this experience, I thanked God for appearing to me and then I quickly felt the cold sub-degree temperature chill my lightly clothed physical body as I immediately dashed to the house pondering what all that was about.

The message was delivered with great love and concern for humanity, but why was I the one to receive it? I was in no position to be able to influence those in power to change their ways to more loving ways. **I am just one ordinary woman!** I have no influence over governments or terrorists. So why did the Light-God reveal that information to *me*? How could I do anything? Who would listen? I was, and still am, confused about this. Perhaps my role in all this was a simple one. Perhaps I was being asked to put as much positive (loving) energy out into my own little corner of the world, and through the books I write. Perhaps this was all I was personally being asked to do.

After about an hour sitting on the sofa in the living room and contemplating what had just happened, I crawled into that warm bed and fell asleep peacefully, knowing that what I experienced was another REAL visitation by the Light-God. I still struggle with the question, "*Why me?*" I guess I will never know that answer. Perhaps God is bringing messages of love to humanity through ordinary, simple people to show us that God is still with us today, and can continue to speak to us in modern times, with the desire to help us.

Certainly, I have no ego agenda to make myself holier than thou or more deserving than anyone else. I absolutely **do not** want to glorify myself; I only want to inspire others to lift their hearts upward and inwardly to their own Divine reality so that they can have a more powerful and intimate relationship with the One who loves all of us **equally**. I only want to pass along the messages that the Light-God has revealed to me to share with others. I promised I would do this. I am not the message; I'm just a microphone that echoes God's Love to those who will listen, that's all. You should not revere the messenger, only the message which comes from the Love of God.

4

COMING BACK

My Beloved,
All your works are an expression of My Enabling. When you realize this, you will become humbled knowing that you are dependent upon Me for everything.

In what can only be regarded as synchronicity, three months following my 1979 near-death-like experience, I read in a local newspaper that there was going to be a book review of Dr. Raymond Moody's book, *Life after Life*, at a local church. I was not a member of that church, but something deep within me whispered to me, *Nancy, you must attend that church lecture.* I went to the church that night not really knowing why I felt the need to go. After all, I had never heard of that doctor or his book or gone to that church. I simply followed my intuition.

Seated around the table were twelve men and women and the minister. All the people were members of that church, so I felt somewhat uneasy being a perfect stranger. The minister passed some paperback books around the table to each of us. The title intrigued me, *Life after Life*, but

I had no idea what the book was about. I flipped a few pages to read some sentences before the meeting started. When I saw some sentences that a near-death experiencer in the book reported, I became so excited that I boldly exclaimed joyously to the group,

"This is what happened to me! I experienced the same thing! Oh my goodness, this is what happened to me!"

The people seated around the table looked at me without saying anything. I wondered if any of them had read Dr. Moody's book before, or even knew anything about the experience that Dr. Moody, in his book, termed a near-death experience. Those few pages I glanced at was the very first time I learned that others had experienced what I did. I can't begin to tell you how overwhelmed I was to learn that. It was as if God had deliberately led me by intuition to attend that small church meeting to enable me to learn about near-death experiences.

The minister leaned over the table looking straight into my tearful eyes and said,

"Nancy, why don't you share with the group what happened to you."

Thus became my first undertaking to speak publicly about both my near-death experience in the early 1960's and my 1979 near-death-like experience. I recall telling the group that I wasn't close to death during my 1979 experience; I was delivering a eulogy. I could see the group was confused, but they began to ask questions which I quickly answered as best I could. The minister filled in a lot of the blanks with information from Dr. Moody's book so the group and I could understand more what this spiritually transformative experience entailed.

After the meeting was over, the minister came up to me and held me, thanking me for having the courage to share my experiences with the group. I cried softly, feeling the love and support I received from the minister and the group. It was overwhelming for me to know that someone believed what I was trying to articulate, often times, stumbling for words. It was within those pages of Moody's book where I first learned the word, "ineffable," meaning there are no words adequate to describe the experience. That word popped out from the pages of the book imprinting on my mind the truth of what I had been trying to express to the group, but could not adequately articulate. It was very re-assuring to know that others who had experiences with a Being of Light also could not convey their own life-transforming event satisfactorily. I was not alone!

Driving home from that meeting, I was so overwhelmed by the support I had received that evening from everyone. I made a promise to God that I would do something to help others and to support them as I had been supported that night. I had no idea what I would do, but I knew that there must be many people who had this type of experience who also needed to be supported. I asked God to help me figure out how I would be able to help others in this way and then I just left it up to God to bring this about for me if that was what I was supposed to do.

Within a few months following that church meeting, I noticed some television interviews with individuals who had near-death experiences and experts who discussed this topic. The primary discussion at that time was between skeptics and advocates of these experiences, with each one trying to explain what was the cause or not the cause of near-death experiences.

But this is decidedly a secular world of academia. For example, pertaining to the NDE researchers, some re-searchers do not stray far from the prevailing orthodoxy in their given fields. For instance, psychologists or psychiatrists may focus on psychological explanations for the cause of transcendent type of experiences. Physiologists or neuroscientists may want to explain it in terms of neurons in the brain misfiring, and so forth. Some thought the cause to be hallucinations, oxygen deprivation to the brain, anesthesia, drugs, and so many other theories. When I saw those interviews with many well-known and intelligent men and women, I became frustrated with their theories to explain the cause of NDEs.

You see, during the time I was delivering a eulogy and had an identical experience to a near-death experience, I was definitely not hallucinating. I did not have oxygen deprivation to the brain, as I was functioning normally while delivering a eulogy. I was not under anesthesia, and I was not on any drugs whatsoever. I was 38 years old, mentally stable and physically healthy, working as a cancer researcher at a major university, raising a loving family, and being a community leader and a contributing member of society. So any explanation those "experts" were claiming to be the cause of near-death experiences were nullified, in my opinion. *If only they would interview me to see that their opinions were wrong*, I thought. It is my opinion that innovations are made through free inquiry, when we can open our minds to other perspectives outside the narrow confines of the scientific mainstream community.

Although to this day there are many theories of the cause of these experiences, no one has been able to prove a particular cause. Each theory has been shot down by the research so far.

Having had four personal transcendent experiences with the Light-God during my life, it is my personal opinion that the answers to those questions will not be found anywhere in modern science. I propose that the answers will be derived from the individual experiencers themselves, who will lead us on our search for the answers about the mystery of our true nature.

William James, an American philosopher and psychologist, Harvard trained physician, 1842-1910, once said,

"If you want to upset the law that all crows are black, you mustn't seek to show that no crows are; it is enough if you prove one single crow to be white."

Well, ladies and gentlemen, my 1979 near-death-like experience is that white crow in the midst of all black crows within the field of near-death experiences. One white crow can disprove the law that all crows are black. Hmm. Think about it. An albino white crow feeds the same way black crows feed; it flies the same way; it reproduces the same way; there is no difference. Not only is my near-death-like experience a "white crow" by virtue of having the same components as a near-death experience, there are many others like me who have had experiences that mimic near-death experiences while not coming close to death, suffering serious illness, or enduring physical trauma. There are many black *and* white crows experiencing the same phenomena!

It became apparent to me that those experts in their fields did not have the complete picture of what this type of experience entails, nor did they want to include those experiences in their research studies. They were only interested in studying the black crows – near-death experiences.

So began my quest to try to bring attention to the type of experience I had while delivering a eulogy. It was identical in form and content to a near-death experience. Surely, it was an important piece of the mysterious puzzle of consciousness and the nature of reality. I knew that I must try to bring information about my eulogy experience to those who were in a position to investigate near-death experiences so we can have a better understanding of human life and its purpose.

It became my passion to alert others that coming close to death is only one trigger, and apparently my own experience proved that there are other triggers as well. To make matters worse, there wasn't even a term given to my type of experience at that time. I wondered who would listen to me, since the interest was only focused on near-death experiences. I had to try however.

One morning during the early 1980's, I turned the television on and the Phil Donahue talk show was winding down its last minute. On the stage were several guests that Phil described as near-death experiencers. *Oh darn, I missed a good program*. I thought. Then Phil Donahue said,

"*If anyone would like to contact our guest speaker, Professor Kenneth Ring, PhD, Psychology professor at the University of Connecticut who is doing research on near-death experiences, here is his contact information.*"

His contact information appeared on the screen and I immediately wrote it down thinking one day I should contact him and tell him I had an experience identical to a near-death experience, only I wasn't close to death at the time. I had second thoughts about doing that, however. I mean, he was a professor of psychology, for goodness' sake. He probably would think I was crazy. No one had ever mentioned my type of experience before, so what would be the chance that Professor Ring would believe me?

But it didn't take me long to push past my reluctance and write a letter to Dr. Ring describing my experience. Within a few days, I received a letter back asking that we converse by phone about my experience, which we did. Dr. Ring then asked my permission to include portions of my letter describing my experience in a book he was working on, *Heading Toward Omega: In Search of the Meaning of the Near-Death Experience*, which was published in 1984. He was so enthralled that I wrote to him because he had already written seven chapters in his book (unknown to me at the time) when my letter arrived, and it seemed to be an outline of his book. In his book, he wrote in part, "*Nancy Clark's letter is valuable chiefly not because it so well exemplifies the typical life transformations in NDErs but because it shows that these same transformations do not depend on having NDEs.*"

I was elated that finally someone had listened to me and knew that my experience was every bit as important to learn from as near-death experiences. Dr. Ring has the distinction of being the very first near-death experience researcher who applied strict research methodology to his work. His first book, *Life at Life* is a brilliant and extensive study of NDEs. After his research work gained credible recognition from others, scientific research in the field emerged and continues to this day.

Dr. Ring was a voice for me when I was powerless to be that voice for myself. Eventually, my own voice became a voice for so many others who had experiences similar to NDEs through my talks, the books I have written, and the study I launched of ordinary people having spiritually trans-formative experiences.

I also continue to encourage the researchers to take a closer look at experiences that mimic NDEs. Eventually, a term for my type of experience entered the research literature and is currently called a *near-death-like experience*. As time passed, this type of experience was written up in the books of several researchers, such as PMH Atwater, Ken Ring, and others. Additionally, it is recognized by the International Association for Near-Death Studies, Inc., giving the general public more information about these experiences that mimic the NDE.

Ken Ring, along with Raymond Moody, John Audette, and Bruce Greyson, M.D. were the founders of an organization called IANDS (International Association for Near-Death Experiences). Kenneth Ring was the president, and in 1984, he invited me to consider forming a local chapter of IANDS in Columbus, Ohio where I live. I immediately knew that was a way for me to honor the promise I had made to God that evening in 1979 while driving home from that church meeting. This would be a wonderful opportunity to give other experiencers the support they may need after finding themselves returning to a physical realm, where it can be sometimes difficult to share this experience with family or friends. So, I formed a local chapter of IANDS in 1984. Today, our group remains the second longest surviving IANDS chapter in the entire world. I continue to serve as it's facilitator to this day.

IANDS is a world-wide non-profit organization devoted to the encouragement of research, education, and support of individuals who have had near-death and similar experiences. The organization has over fifty local groups throughout the world. It holds international conferences, workshops, and retreats, and provides a wealth of educational material for its members, the media, and the general public. It also produces a quarterly peer-reviewed professional journal and newsletter on the subject of near-death experiences. More information about this organization can be found online at www.iands.org.

It is my hope that no one reading this book will allow prejudice or cynicism to interfere with the benefits they might receive, because as God is my witness, I will never fabricate or embellish upon that which was given to me by Grace.

Rest assured, it isn't my purpose to convert anyone to my way of believing. Rather, I simply hope to encourage people to see that yes, seeing is believing, but also, believing is a form of seeing. If I can inspire others to realize that the eternal expression of Divine Love is within each person, purifying ourselves to receive what is truly ours, then the wisdom that my Great Teacher, the Light-God, revealed to me will be the greatest gift I can, in turn, give to others.

I honor the calling I was given. I know with a certainty clearer than anything else in my life that it is something I intend to do – I must do! Nothing ignites my passion the way this calling has. It is my North Star, demanding more and more of me, magnetizing me to live a life greater than my own, and fulfilling my own at the same time.

For my service to the Light and to my fellowman, I will not take advantage of anyone for ulterior purposes. The love I feel for my Great Teacher, the Light-God, is an ever-present gratitude for having been granted the gift of experiencing the Presence of God. In serving others, I am returning my love to the Creator in gratitude for what I have been given. As a result, I am willing to surrender all ego motives, except to fulfill my promise to serve God. That is my ultimate destiny.

My desire is to help others as I have been helped. As Light pours forth and fills each being whose heart and mind are open to receive it, the dark nature of ourselves can become dissolved by the Light. A love so great, so pure, so beautiful that you cannot imagine the potential it has to lift one's consciousness above hatred, fear, or jealousy so that all suffering can cease within the individual. Divine Grace calls us to know the Divine nature of ourselves, as well as every man, woman and child in the universe. As we let the Light shine in our minds, the way is made clear, for only through love will we lift humanity and awaken to the joy of being human.

What I have just written is perhaps the most relevant aftereffect of my near-death-like, spiritually transformative experience. I feel an intense connection with the Divine Presence in my daily life. The gifts I have received must be given to the world- those truths which my Great Teacher, the Light, blessed me with. I cannot sit back and not do this. It is my passion, my destiny.

During my life preview, the Light showed me visions of what my life would be like upon my return to physical consciousness. My entire circle of friends would move out of my life because they feared I was mentally unstable because I spoke about my experiences with them. Remember, it was early 1979 and the general public had not yet learned much about these experiences, so it is understandable why my friends were uneasy with me. I also saw in that vision that I would gain an entire new circle of friends who were more spiritually similar to the new person I became.

Well, I did lose my entire circle of friends, and I did draw new friends who were more spiritually similar to me. I love my dear friends who support and love me for the person I became, while having no ill will against my former friends.

During my life preview, I was also shown visions of speaking before audiences, and some people would snicker or their body language revealed they thought that what I was speaking about was pure lunacy. Some people in the audience got up from their chairs and walked out. The subject of near-death experiences was still in its infancy as far as the general public was concerned, so it was to be expected that talk of experiencing an afterlife and returning from it would be regarded with skepticism. My life preview of this skeptical attitude among many people helped me to understand what

I was up against and what I needed to do in order to educate the public about these experiences.

I was also shown how many people listening to my talks would become inspired. I saw many little red hearts symbolically being lifted up, up, toward the Light.

During my life preview, I also saw how my entire family would disbelieve my experiences. No matter what I said, they always felt there was some logical explanation for what I experienced, and that I didn't really have transcendent experiences. I was never able to convince them otherwise. After reading my letters that I sent home that talked about my experience with the Light-God, my father told my mother,

"I don't want to read any more of Nancy's letters. All she does is talk about seeing God and how she has been changed. Well, I just want our old Nancy back again, the way I have always known her."

My father was true to his word. He never read any more of my letters that I sent to my parents.

That may sound terrible and you may assume that my feelings were hurt or that I became sad or angry that my family, the ones who are supposed to be in your corner no matter what, were not supporting me. But that was not how I felt. I deeply respected their right to their own opinion. I didn't try to push my agenda onto anyone.

You see, that life preview was given to me so that I would know with certainty what my "calling" would entail, both the positive and the negative aspects. The Light-God made me look at those scenes so that I would be certain of the decision before me. Did I want to chicken out and say no to God because people didn't believe me and ridiculed me? Or did I want to accept the calling no matter what I had to endure? I didn't have to think about the decision I would make. My love for God was so intense that I wanted to devote myself completely to God, who wanted to entrust me with such glorious spiritual truths to share with others.

I said, "*Yes, God, I will serve until I draw my final breath. I am yours!*"

I have not found it difficult to integrate my experiences into my life. I believe the life preview that I was given allowed me to understand that no matter what I would go through, I chose to accept my destiny with love. When love is present, it wipes out fear. It negates ego's desire to pull me away from my destiny. There have been other changes in me when I returned from my experience.

I became less materialistic, more loving, more forgiving, and definitely more spiritual than religious. Helping others has become very meaningful for me. I no longer have the fear of death. According to the research, it is common for experiencers to report they no longer have the fear of death. I continue to live each day in the joy of knowing that I have a purpose yet to fulfill, and when that purpose has been fulfilled, there will be no fear of approaching death, only the joy and awareness of love calling me "home" again.

My self-esteem increased dramatically. I feel a very close bond with nature. Wild animals in the forest have approached me, perhaps sensing the love that I am feeling for them.

The following is a true story. One day I was sitting on a log in the woods, drawing my love from Heaven above and sending my love back to Heaven. The songs of the birds were being heard in the trees above my head; the wildflowers were peaking their heads above the golden leaves that lay on the ground. Surely, I am in Heaven sitting right there on a decaying log as I saw the perfection of God's goodness in the beauty and glory of His creation.

Soon, a raccoon appeared in the distance and began walking toward me. I smiled and figured that as soon as he would see me, he would scurry away. He didn't. Instead, he kept walking toward me, unafraid of me. I just sat there, quietly watching him as he approached me until he stopped at my feet and looked straight into my eyes. For one quiet moment, I opened my heart to this little fellow, and it felt as if he did the same. What happened next took my breath away.

Edging himself closer to my feet, he grasped my leg and started to climb. Slowly and steadily, he climbed to my shoulder and sat down. His soft paws began playing with my hair and then he playfully covered my eyes with his paws, as if playing peek-a-boo with me. He finally decided it was his time to take his nap, so he settled down and fell asleep right there on my shoulder for an hour.

I didn't want to disturb him from his nap, so I remained sitting on the log with a glow in my heart that brought such sweetness flowing through my body. In that stillness, my whole body was at peace, feeling the warmth of his body against mine, and listening to the quiet rhythm of his and my own breathing. It was a gentle reminder of what I experienced with the Light-God, that in the Heavenly state of love, all creatures are of God, and belong to this one universal life from which no tiny part can be separated. All are, indeed, one in this Divine Spirit.

In talking more about the changes that took place in me following my experiences, I became more intuitive and I'm able to be at peace more easily. I am able to feel someone's emotions as if those emotions were my own. This is known as clairsentience. I have many pre-cognitive type dreams that foretell the future; for instance, I witnessed during a dream, the explosion of the spacecraft Challenger, exactly the form of the explosion that happened after liftoff. Two days later, Challenger exploded after liftoff exactly how I perceived it during my dream. I have also had visions of people dying and within a short period of time, usually days or a few weeks, they did indeed die. I also have many after-death communication experiences, (ADCs).

Gratitude and honesty are values that I hold most dear. I find it very difficult when people lie, disrespect, or deceive others in any way. I also dislike small talk, preferring to talk about deeper and more meaningful topics. No to loud noises, hard rock music, preferring instead to listen to opera, elevator music, and soft New Age music. Electrical sensitivities are problematic for me, as most of the time I affect my computer with the energy emitting from me. My energy does weird things with my computer to frustrate me because I don't know how to fix what I've messed up. It is a good thing that I have two dear friends who are computer gurus that I can call to help me. They are a blessing from Heaven to come to my aid when I face such challenges.

5

THE NATURE OF GOD

My Beloved,
I will lead you in a Spirit-led direction into a deeper
fellowship with Me, deeper than you could ever have
imagined. I want you to know Me, not just about Me.
Take my Hand and I will lead you into My Light.

It is very scary to step outside the teachings of our parents or our religions when they talk about God. Because our parents love us and wouldn't intentionally deceive us, we trust them. We believe that they are telling us the truth about God and what to believe. We are also taught that those who are among the religious clergy, who have been schooled in religious doctrine, are the authority figures who know more about God than we do. We are taught to trust them, for they have our spiritual lives to develop and protect.

But what is so heartbreaking is that we are taught to fear God, and that God is a very vengeful God who sits up in Heaven watching every move we make, and then keeps score of everything we do. Chalk up good points for good behavior, bad points for bad behavior. Those points then determine whether God will welcome us into Heaven or throw us away into a fiery pit of hell after we die. Or we are taught of our unworthiness before being taught how much God loves us and wants the very best for us. On the one hand, God is a vindictive, punishing God, but on the other hand, a loving one at the same time. Are you scratching your head at this time wondering what gives?

I know that is what I was taught as a devout Catholic, and I believed that whatever came from the lips of a priest was absolute truth. I had no other foundation with which to trust and build upon. I did not doubt or question anything. So it isn't any wonder that many others have accepted this way of thinking, often times without questioning. Who wants to risk changing one's long held beliefs about a judgmental, punishing God if that means they may not go to Heaven but be sent to hell instead? Even if they have an inner feeling that God surely can't be like that, many will continue to hold onto their beliefs because they do not want to risk God's so-called wrath that may be imposed on them after death. Or they may just throw in the towel and no longer want any part of religion and/or God.

Thousands of near-death experiencers including myself, have reported having a life review while in the presence of God, and they consistently talk of a God of *unconditional* love, one who is not judging us to be good or bad, and who has no strings attached to that Divine Love for us. Each individual is loved no more, no less, than anyone else. Each is cherished beyond human comprehension! Oh boy, this knowledge- coming from the mouths of so many people who have died or nearly died or who were in God's Presence through other means and witnessed what life on the other side of the veil is like – makes a lot of religious people angry. Some call these witnesses to life on the other side of the veil with God, "followers of Satan," because of a passage they refer to in the Bible that says, "*Satan can be disguised as an angel of Light.*"

I remember, a few months following my mystical union with the Light-God, a minister who I was talking to about my experience, told me I must never speak again of my experience because Satan was working through me. I was stunned! I was fully expecting this man of God to support me and to be happy that God took an ordinary woman like me, and instantly transformed my life. By Divine Grace, I was given a cherished gift. It was not a gift to keep to myself, but a gift to be given to all humanity, with my whole heart, with all my mind, and with my entire soul. But that was not the minister's agenda. He continued to preach how I must rebuke my experience or else suffer the consequences of hell when I die.

Thoughts of my own hard-held religious beliefs, from prior to my Sacred union with the Light-God allowed me to have compassion for this minister. After all, he was trying to help someone who he believed was a lost soul, to regain favor with God by declaring my experience the work of the devil, so that in rebuking my experience, I would be saved.

I responded to the minister by saying,

"*If it were Satan working through me, wouldn't Satan do everything in his power to lead me **away** from God? My experience brought me **to** God, and I intend to stay there, witnessing to the miracle of God's Love for all of us.*"

I continued, "*I will always speak of what God did for me until I draw my final breath because that is what God called me to do — 'to speak and to write' what God had revealed to me.*"

The minister just shook his head, and as he was walking away, he said,

"I will pray for your salvation."

Not unlike most folks indoctrinated in traditional religion, my view of God was a male figure with a long white beard and a long white robe who sat on a throne in a place called Heaven. That image was shattered once I was in the presence of the Light-God when I was called to Heaven's door. Light! Light! Light! Glorious, crystal pure Light, unlike anything in the physical dimension or the entire cosmos. A *Being* of Light, Universal Consciousness, which permeates all form underlying the universe, Energy, Love, Power, and Peace, was what I understood God to be, all that, and more.

My Great Teacher began my lessons with unspoken knowingness. Remember, I mentioned previously, that there was no separation between the Creator and me. Because my ego was not present during the entire experience, there was no chance of misinterpreting what my Great Teacher was communicating to me. I understood everything that I was learning through *non-verbal* communication. However, in writing about these teachings I received from the Light, I will have to use my words carefully, so as to remain true to what I learned through non-verbal communication.

This statement began my lesson with God:

"I am Love; therefore, anyone who knows love, knows Me."

Let that sink in, folks. God is Love, pure and simple. God is everywhere and permeates everything. God is beyond perception or form, yet present and innate within all form. God is Divine Energy that is the Creator of All There Is, and besides all the many qualities that God has, God has a wonderful personality. Yes, the Being of Light-God revealed a most tender and intimate *"relationship"* with me, cherishing me as God's child and friend. I could have snuggled in the arms of God for eternity; that's how cherished I felt, as if there were no barriers between God and my own Divine nature that was being revealed to me. We were One.

The Light was loving me with such a vibration so refined, like a jewel, shining and bright, casting its brilliance deep within my being. I knew that my individual Divine nature was not separate from God's Divine Nature. That opened a new awareness of my Oneness with God, a truth that would follow me all the remaining days of my life. But God was quick to remind me that the Creator's Love **shines equally on all, and is not reserved for the favored few.** This is the reason why I am so passionate about helping others to comprehend this, so they may accept this Sacred Love which is the miracle we have been given to enrich our lives and the lives of others – no strings attached. It is freely given to all. I was overjoyed to learn that there is no hierarchy involved in God's unconditional love for all of us and that it will never be taken away from us for any reason whatsoever.

Many people perceive God to be a tyrannical cruel punisher who is to be blamed for everything, from tornados, earthquakes, diseases, conflicts between men and nations, to anything that can go wrong with human nature. In essence, the Creator was allowing me to understand that God was getting a "raw deal." God wanted me to understand that God's unconditional, unimaginable love is given freely to every living human being and to every plant and animal as well. In fact, everything that God created is loved, because God is Love. That is God's nature. God is never the opposite of love – never! If a loving God were causing human conflict in any way, then God would be something other than Love. But God is Love! **Humans cause their own suffering, not God!**

I had many light-bulb moments during my Oneness with the Light-God, and one of them during my lessons was the understanding that God doesn't require that we love God in order for God to love us. We will not be punished or have blessings withdrawn from us because we may be an atheist, or if we do not choose to love God. It's God's nature to love us no matter who we are or what we have done, period, finis, end of story!

During my experience, I understood that there was no fiery burning pit of hell that God condemns us to following our death. I did understand, however, that the absence or separation of love and Light encountered by one's soul was a torment that for me, personally, would be unimaginable.

God does not dispose of us for eternity like a bag of garbage if we have sinned or made mistakes in our life. Please understand that. God loves each and every one of us beyond our human comprehension! I cannot emphasize that enough. I cannot underscore how cherished we are, and the warmth, the tenderness, and the all-encompassing concern God has for each of us. I cannot stress enough how the enfolding power of the Light's Love is nearer to us than our breath. We live in the Light's heart and the Light lives in ours, for all eternity. How many times must I repeat this so you will believe this?

Okay, I can already hear the silent questions being asked by the reader.

"*What happens to the Hitlers of our world, those who are evil and do horrendous harm to others? They have to be punished! They must suffer in return for the harm they have done to others. Surely, they are the ones who will be sent to hell by a just God.*"

I stand by what I have always said; God's love for us is unconditional, no matter what we have done with our earthly lives. It would be unjust for God to be two-faced, acting loving one time, then unloving, another time. Unconditional love means no strings attached! Unconditional love doesn't keep score. Unconditional love doesn't inflict guilt or punishment. Unconditional love teaches, helps, guides.

"Sin" is simply a mistake, that's all. Mistakes need to be learned from, corrected, and not to be repeated. If we haven't learned from our mistakes, then our life experiences will bring them right back to us until we do learn them.

What parent would send their child to a place of torment because they made a mistake? You would still love them no matter what they did. Of course you would want them to take responsibility, learn from and make amends for their mistakes and you would want to help guide them to a better life. Well, not to fault any parent, but God loves your children more than you love them! That may sound impossible, but it is true. God's love for every single one of us is totally ineffable, and beyond our imagination. Be glad that we have such a loving, forgiving, compassionate Creator who loves us so much!

Because we have been taught to love *conditionally*, we cannot fully understand what unconditional love is. That is why we want bad people to be punished and suffer in hell for eternity. Conditional love serves our ego needs, while unconditional love is pure, and is of God.

Some souls do find themselves in a hellish realm, and it was my understanding that souls enter the realm that is *compatible with their particular spiritual vibration*. I do recall very clearly that God wants every soul to be with God because we are so loved. Yes, even the Hitlers of the world – *everyone*. God's Love for even the most abominable individual is steadfast and unchanging. With great clarity, the message I was being given was that God's perfect Love will give every soul every opportunity to come "home" when that soul is ready and willing. If we have not evolved enough spiritually, we will be given every opportunity to learn love's lessons through the many realms that exist on the other side.

I "saw" around eleven different dimensions as the Light was traveling with me through the dark universe. However, I did not see in the manner we humans see phenomena with our eyes; my vision had instead transcended the boundaries of matter. I was not tied by man's visible concepts of time or space. Rather, the inner sanctuary of my being drew its knowledge from the Divine Source that I had been transformed into. Everything that was happening was loaded with infinite meaning as the secrets of the universe were being revealed to me.

The different realms are like school. We learn and advance to the next level, increasing our spiritual vibration until we graduate and reach Heaven where our vibrational energy is compatible with the Light.

I also understood that there are always angels or guides around all souls to help them advance toward the Light when the soul is ready. We are never alone.

6

THE SOUL

My Beloved,
The inner Light of My Love envelops, enlightens,
enriches, and purifies you. If you allow it to come forth
through you it can be delivered to the world.

What is the soul? I grew up thinking the soul was something inside the physical body of a person, just sitting there, doing nothing. I believed my soul's purpose was simply to exit my body upon death, and it went to either Heaven or hell, depending, of course, on whether my soul was worthy to enter Heaven based on how good a life I had led. As you can see, I didn't understand the soul at all. That is, until I had my near-death and near-death-like/mystical, spiritually transformative experiences.

Because I actually died during childbirth and experienced still being "alive" in the presence of the Light-God, in a different form and different dimension (other than the physical realm,) it wasn't a great stretch for me to know it was my soul that had exited my physical body when I died. That confirmed my beliefs as I described earlier. But it wasn't until my near-death-like experience seventeen years later, when I entered Heaven with the Light-God again, that my understanding of the soul evolved to an advanced level. Then, a new world of discernment of the soul was made known to me. That understanding was one of the lessons my Great Teacher, the Light, wanted me to comprehend. I must admit, that knowledge was never in my consciousness to begin with. So I was a blank slate for the Light to teach me.

I am aware that some people use the terms "soul" and "spirit" interchangeably. Some define "soul" as "mind" and define "spirit" as our Higher Self. For the purposes of my own interpretation, I refer to "soul" or "spirit" as our Higher Self or the Divine aspect of ourselves. I also make a distinction between our Divine Higher Self and our lower self as "ego," or personality-self. You may or may not agree with me.

Yes, it is true that the soul resides within the physical body during its lifetime, then exits the body at the time of death to continue life in another dimension. We cannot know the soul through the physical senses. We cannot see, touch, smell, taste, or hear it, because those features are the product of the human mind, of mortal, finite senses. Soul is the essence or the energy of life itself, and here's the revelation that was unknown to me previously. The soul is that part of the Light-God residing within each and every person. Actually, it is accurate to say that we *are* a soul who *has* a personality or ego, and it is this personality-self that is our instrument of expression in the world. But generally, what happens to us is that our personality-selves get so focused on ourselves, driving us to see only the material world and thinking only of ourselves and our own needs, that the soul isn't given the time or space to express itself.

But when the personality-self or the ego chooses to purify itself and invites the soul to express itself, then and only then do we recognize the Divine Light within, our purpose, and a profound sense of inspiration and joy. Soul encourages us to become our best selves, to come to the fullness of life, to the flowering of our unique gifts, and to be the expression of our true self, the holy self, the completed self.

I recall during my near-death-like experience that I was rejoicing in knowing I was being allowed to experience the presence of God. As indescribable as that was, my soul began to understand at a very deep level that the Light-God is the inner essence of everything, object, or person. All that is created and has existence shares in reflecting the glory and divinity of the Divine. Nothing is better or worse than anything else, nor is it of different value or significance.

Fresh new truths permeated my consciousness with wonderful feelings of love that lifted me into a new and expanded awareness. I understood the soul to be the fulfillment of God, and that we are that place in consciousness where God shines through.

But it is hard to describe the soul, just as it is hard to describe the essence of the Creator. The best I can do is to share what my Great Teacher revealed to me about the *power* of the soul.

The soul is Divine Love. It wants us to remember who we are at the core of our being, something we have forgotten. We are a Divine Being, endowed with the attributes of the Creator. It is the soul's purpose to self-express its Divine nature freely, inwardly and outwardly, ultimately bearing the fruits of love, understanding, and compassion within the individual. To the degree that we learn to live from our true identity, our sufferings will be replaced with peace and wisdom.

Just think of the gift we humans were given when we were born into this world as a soul housed in our physical bodies, and to know that our soul will stay with us for eternity. Just as no two fingerprints or two snowflakes are identical, our soul is what makes us different and unique from every other soul in the universe!

When we are working *with* our soul, we become a radiant soul shining through its material body. The expression of soul through us reveals an iridescent, beautiful, sterling spirit which illuminates and reveals life in all its truth and simplicity. Flinging open the doors of life for us, it brings us into touch with a gladness which is the Spirit of Joy and spells kinship with God. It expands our potential and fulfills our highest destiny. Without this guiding consciousness, the spiritual knowledge we receive would be of little use.

It is the soul which recognizes the Truth, which knows and feels that it is the Truth. Accepting, it reaches the stage of inward conviction which enables it to manifest its Divine attributes. We know beyond a shadow of a doubt that inner peace will come as we turn to the spiritual consciousness of life rather than depending upon the material sense of man and the universe. We then become our own authority as we experience this wonderful change within and without. We learn to overcome the sense of struggle over worldly affairs as we enter the realm of heavenly affairs found deep within the Divine Spirit within.

I recall the time our house burned down. The house quickly filled with thick, dark smoke as flames of hot, searing intensity threatened our safety. My family escaped unharmed, finding our way to safety outdoors. Even as I was crawling on the floor to escape breathing in the deadly smoke, I had no fear of the possibility of dying in the fire. Something triggered my spiritual consciousness to lift my vision from the human condition, which resulted in a greater gift of feeling the actual presence of God within. My intuitive voice within was so great that I could hear God whispering His love throughout my being. I was able to relax and let outside things drop away. This inner message of lasting peace enabled me to deal with the challenges that faced our family in rebuilding our lives after the fire.

Perfect love, welling up from the center of one's being, flows without interruption, as long as one remains in a peaceful attitude. In the midst of the Divine Love which is the soul, I was no longer at the mercy of fear when our house was destroyed. A fog of muddled thoughts, which could have easily enmeshed me more than ever in perplexity, was absent. When others learned of our house being destroyed by fire, they automatically assumed that I was devastated by the loss. As curious as it may seem, I was not. My family was a wreck, but I had found inner peace as we picked up the pieces of our lives and moved on.

My soul's voice had liberated me to be able to surmount all the obstacles our house fire manifested for us in the physical sense. It was guiding me to what I needed to do. Soul was my anchor to show me what I am in potentiality, and my burdens were not burdens, but really tests of character.

The Light-God taught me that our soul knows that we are never alone. There is no separation; there is only oneness with the Divinity of All that has or ever will be created. The soul is our state of consciousness that enables us to rest from the stresses of the outer material world to stand back of ourselves and see God at work.

What a God-sent blessing we have been given to be able to allow our soul to blossom and bear fruit of the Spirit, so that humanity can be aligned in the oneness of God and to know the hand of God in action in our daily lives!

It is true that this heavenly soul consciousness results in a more harmonious human life, because this power cannot be felt unless we realize love in its deepest meaning. Only by living from our soul body can we grasp its intrinsic value. Soul will reveal its wisdom, and we will know and feel that it is the truth.

We have mistaken the intellect for the soul and have tried to obtain wisdom by our minds alone. Yes, it is true that knowledge is obtainable in this manner, but it is the soul who has the key to wisdom. Until we recognize that we hold the key to opening the soul's wisdom, it will remain closed. This is our individual choice, to awaken to the call of the soul or not to awaken. What do I mean by awakening to the call of the soul? I mean the growth of the personality, of character, and spirituality, whereby one is able to work with Divine Intent in all aspects of one's life.

My Great Teacher taught me that all living things are working out a part of the Divine plan which is vastly more important than we can conceive of. We are so focused on our five senses as means of perception, and that results in our being constricted by matter and inhibited by suffering, misunderstanding, and emotion. With all that distraction going on, our soul cannot reach the mind unless that mind has learned to open itself up to receive the higher realizations, brought through consciousness from soul. Through intuition, inspiration, and love, soul can make itself recognizable to the mind the tremendous resources that we can utilize for abundant living.

The soul is our higher self that watches over our personality-self, waiting for the invitation to experience itself outwardly. Think of it this way: When contact with the soul has been made, it is like the mind touching a live wire. Working like an electric current, the mind has tuned in to a new world of ideas that is known to the soul. That's when things begin to happen! The power of Divinity flows

our inner connection *ignore*

through, guiding, helping, protecting, and preparing for the wonders ahead. But when we break that contact, it is as though our wire has gone dead. The connecting link or relationship between spirit and our human personality cannot function perfectly and we are once again thrown back upon our lesser resources.

Do we have freewill? My understanding was that we are born into this world having pre-determined experiences that will teach us the lessons we want to learn throughout our life. Our soul has the aspirations to reveal itself to accelerate its growth so it will ultimately find its Oneness in God. The soul, once it has entered the physical body of a human, will always be guiding us to make the right choices so that our soul's destiny will be realized.

If we don't like the challenges of our life experiences that our soul has pre-determined that we work through, can we use our free will to change things and create what we desire instead? Perhaps we don't want to be poor or sick or anything else that will cause our suffering. Yes, we can make choices in our life, but no matter how hard we may want to alter our destiny, it won't happen. Our soul came here to fulfill that destiny, and it will do just that. We will continue to draw experiences to ourselves until we learn the lesson or lessons we came here to work out. We should embrace those experiences, quickly learning the lessons from those experiences instead of dragging them out or postponing them with choices that will temporarily not allow us to learn those lessons.

I remember some time ago I saw a television interview with Christopher Reeve, the actor who played Superman. After his horrendous accident, which left him a quadriplegic, he announced to the interviewer that his accident was the best thing that ever happened to him. Why? He said his spirituality blossomed as a result. He said he became more loving, and compassionate, and wanted to serve others, and had it not been for that accident, he wouldn't have become the loving person he became. He said that if he had it to do all over again, he would not have changed a thing! That's powerful coming from someone who, seemingly, had a very affluent life and a great career. It was his accident that changed the course of his life into a more meaningful one for him.

Most of us would not want to go through a life experience as Christopher Reeve went through. But this serves as an example that no matter how difficult our circumstances may appear, there is always an underlying, greater destiny we came into this world to fulfill. We should remain mindful that one person can make a difference in our world to help make it a better place, no matter whether that person has had a tragic life experience or has died.

I would like to tell you about a Brazilian Formula One racecar driver named Senna, considered the world's greatest racecar driver who ever lived. My son and I were watching a race on television in which Senna was racing his car one afternoon. It was the race that would end his life at the age of 34.

The weekend of April 29, 1994 was disastrous not only for Senna, but for other drivers as well. During the qualifying session on Friday, a driver was seriously injured. The next day, another driver was killed when he hit the wall going 190 miles per hour.

Senna's good friend told him to stop racing and go fishing with him instead. But Senna told him he couldn't stop racing.

That Sunday was to be his last race and his final day on earth. Senna spent that morning talking with another driver asking him if he would be willing to help him set up a Grand Prix Drivers Association in order to improve safety in Formula One. Senna had been very concerned about the safety of the drivers and the failure of the racing commission to address the safety issues. The driver agreed to help him.

Once the race began, another driver had an accident, losing a wheel and sending debris into the grandstands, injuring eight people. The race was stopped in order to clear the track. Once the race started again, on lap seven, Senna's car ran off the track at 191 miles per hour and hit a concrete retaining wall. He died at the scene. The cause of the crash was due to a badly designed steering column.

Senna was very religious. That Sunday morning before the race, he read his Bible and told his sister that he was led to a Bible passage that he *"would receive the greatest gift of all, which was God himself."* As it turned out, just seven laps into the race and he was in Heaven with God.

Senna's legacy is that more safety improvements were made in Formula One racing, and no one has been injured since. Many racers can thank him for that. His destiny had been fulfilled at the young age of thirty-four.

I am sure that if Senna had known that his life would end at the young age of thirty-four, he would have wanted to alter that outcome by his "free will," perhaps choosing not to race anymore. His legacy perhaps would then not have been realized. He came into this world for a purpose which was only known to Senna's soul. We can't know what that was. Even though it was suggested to him by his friend to stop racing, Senna listened to his own inner voice suggesting that he should continue racing. It was his soul that carried out his destiny.

Sometimes life is so hard on us that we don't want to go through any more harsh experiences, so we make choices –

our free will – that will lead us away from our true destiny. But those life experiences will keep presenting themselves to us as the challenges we have come here to overcome. We may wish and wish that we can change our destiny, but it won't happen.

A lesson I was taught by my Great Teacher was that God has a plan for His Creation and for our lives. Yes, we were given the freedom to work with this plan or to work against it. Our destiny is meant to accelerate our spiritual growth so that we can be called home, home to our Being, where God and we are One, *SO WE CAN* .... ,....

Nearing the end of my experience, while still being merged into oneness with the Light-God, I was shown all the evils and injustices of the world. Watching over humanity as I did with the Light-God, I felt tremendous love for everyone, even though I witnessed some awful events taking place. I understood that everything was working out the way it was intended according to God's Greater Plan for humanity. I understood that each person was working out, unknowingly, their individual part in the great mysterious puzzle of life, and that the Divine Plan is holy, wise, and benevolent. *PLUS, PLUS, PLUS*

I realize that with all the evil being perpetuated by terrorists, murderers, and the like in our world, we are not easily convinced that there is a wise and benevolent plan that is only known to God. It is too much for our egos to accept this! Even though I remain steadfast as to what God was revealing to me, at times my own ego successfully pulls me away from that truth, and my heart cries out, "*Why is this happening God?*" Because I am human, I can suffer at times, just as everyone suffers when witnessing evil inflicting its atrocious pain onto others. I don't understand some things; I only know that what I experienced with God was truthful.

What I am able to explain, I will, and what I am unable to explain, I will admit that.

Once we can understand that we came into this world to experience the lessons we want to learn, it then becomes easier to take responsibility and make changes in our life. For instance, we may have decided that we want to learn the lesson of forgiveness. Our journey through this life will bring us those opportunities that will help us to learn forgiveness. We may have some people who are in our lives who are downright nasty to us. If we didn't have those individuals in our lives, then how would we learn the lesson of forgiveness if there were no individuals to forgive? Perhaps the motorcycle rider covered from head to toe in tattoos might be here to teach us not to be so judgmental. Or perhaps the slow driver is here to teach us patience.

Can you understand that they came into our life with their behaviors so we could accelerate our soul's growth? If we can take the time to try to determine what the people in our life are trying to teach us, we will find ourselves less apt to over-react in negative ways. If we can go with the flow of life instead of resisting it, we will find ourselves better able to deal with whatever life experiences we will face. As the serenity prayer goes, "*Change the things that can be changed, accept those that cannot, and have the wisdom to know the difference.*"

Sometimes people argue against this way of thinking, saying that if God had intended us to use our God-given nature, He would have given it to us already developed. All life develops as an embryo. We aren't born already mature. So it is with our Spirit's faculties. We evolve; we develop those gifts which are latent within us, bringing into the world our contribution.

It is never a hopeless and futile adventure to seek the

Light; for every difficulty we clear away is so much gained. We aren't given a destiny that is easily accomplished or attainable through our wisdom and resources. It's supposed to be difficult, because that guarantees our reliance upon God – our inner Divine Self to help us. It keeps us close to God. It takes a willingness to ask for help when we find ourselves at crossroads and don't know which road to take. Prayer and meditation are good ways to get in touch with our soul consciousness for guidance. As we trust our inner Divine Voice, it will speak to us and lead us. Our souls were created to benefit us; receive it and accept it, apply it and live it, relish it and rejoice in it!

Our lives are not meant to just show off our intellect and abilities, but to evolve our very souls through which the life force can flow. Something happens to us spiritually when we accept the calling of our soul to unleash the work of the Divine in our life. Our thinking changes. Our motives and goals change. Our desires change. Love, then, becomes the way of unleashing the work of the Divine in our life. This will be made known to us only by following and embracing the path that is congruent with our destiny. Then when we discover the impossible is made possible, we will perceive what God has intended for us to perceive. In that respect, we become a channel for the larger plan of God – to know ourselves as One with our Creator – our truest destiny.

7

REALMS ON THE OTHER SIDE

My Beloved,
When you close your earthly eyes and pass into the
twilight, your Heavenly eyes will be opened and you will
see Me at last. Do not fear coming "home" to Me, my
child. My Loving Arms await your homecoming.

When we die, we are still the same, emotionally, mentally,
spiritually. Our soul has just been released from our physical
body to new life. But what happens to "us" then? At the
moment of death, we are met by family or friends who have
preceded us in death. Sometimes we are greeted by angels,
Jesus, other highly evolved entities, and even animals whose
mission it is to ease the transition from the physical realm
we have just left. We are never alone!

The form we take is, of course, non-physical. However,
we take on the appearance of the physical body we had
when we were alive. Most souls choose their appearance to
be around the age of 30 years or so. Perhaps this is the age
one is most comfortable being. Uncle Ed may have died
at age 95, but in spirit, he will appear to have his youthful

appearance back and will no longer be blind, deaf, or sick in any way. Research data from thousands of near-death experiencers report this. This is great news, isn't it? We will be able to kick up our heels and dance or do cartwheels if we are so inclined, because we will no longer be constricted by our physical bodies.

Our life review, which I will talk about later, will show us the way we lived our life in the physical realm. With clear understanding, we will understand what our soul needs to learn in order to attain our highest spiritual potential. Because our soul consciousness has a desire to develop its innate abilities, it knows that there is truly a purpose to our lives, indeed to life itself. So the soul will be led to the spiritual realm that we have spiritually prepared for and evolved to.

I am being truthful in admitting that I cannot recall what all the different realms or dimensions are specifically. Bits and pieces of my recall is what I will share with the reader. If I am to remember something more of the total knowledge that was "downloaded" into my consciousness while being on the other side, that will happen, perhaps at another time.

Let's continue. My understanding was that the different realms are teaching places to prepare souls to advance to higher, more evolved, spiritual realms. One of the realms I did learn about was one that Christians call "purgatory," where most of us will spend some time. It is here where we will be cleansed of many of our human desires. For those who valued money, power, possessions, even homes they may have been attached to, they may find they are still attached to and longing for them. This is the realm that will help them to rid themselves of those desires, and when that has been completed, the soul will move on to a higher realm.

A rather simple way of understanding this idea of the different realms is to imagine how we evolved intellectually from kindergarten through the different grades in school. We learned as much as we needed in one grade level, and then we moved on to the higher grades for increasing education.

I also recall that there are some realms where we can spend time learning about anything we want to learn about, music, art, languages, and science. I understood that if we wanted to engage in any of that, all we had to do was call it into being with our mind or consciousness. If I wanted to sing like Celine Dion, Pavarotti, or dance like Baryshnikov, I would be able to do so.

This leads me to question, for what purpose does this serve? Is it all for our soul's pleasure, or is this realm a means of preparing the soul for a specific talent or occupation should the soul return to the earth plane? As you can see, even those of us who have experienced ultimate reality still have questions. But once again, I will remind you that I knew everything while I was on the other side, absolutely everything! I just can't recall everything once I came back. Darn!

Prior to my experience, I held firm beliefs that reincarnation was absolutely not a possibility. But immediately upon my return to this physical realm following my experience, I found myself suddenly being open to the idea that it does exist. I do not *remember* having been told that information while on the other side, even though I did receive total knowledge about all things, even the subject of reincarnation. But what changed me? I have to believe that there was something during my experience that allowed me to come back and instantly believe in the *possibility* that reincarnation is real. I am still on the fence with it, but I will say that

I have gone from 0% belief to 60% belief. I am open to the idea.

My point is that it makes sense that some souls are learning their craft on the other side to come to earth to share that gift with us. How many times have we seen a gifted child sing or play a musical instrument so well without any training and we say, "It's a gift straight from God." Maybe it really is! Perhaps that realm that I spoke about earlier is, indeed, preparing souls to bring to earth the many talents and scientific discoveries our physical dimension is in need of. Then those souls reincarnate into our world ready to assist humanity with their gifts. This is speculation on my part, because I don't actually recall the *purpose* of that realm, but intuitively, I am leaning toward this idea.

Remember, those who have been on the other side are given the memory of only a partial knowledge of the spiritual world. It is wrong to assume that their partial knowledge is the total knowledge of the spiritual world.

I do know that the greater our spiritual consciousness, the greater the spiritual realm we will enter. The opposite of that is also true. The lesser our spiritual consciousness, the lower the realm we will enter. My understanding is that those who end up in a lower realm have become so attached to the ego that, temporarily, they don't see the Light of higher planes. The impression or understanding that I had of one particular realm, where some find themselves in cities or in beautiful landscapes, is one of the lower realms. Some souls feel comfortable being in surroundings that remind them of the earth plane, so they go there to gradually get accustomed to being on the other side. They leave that realm once they feel their vibration is being lifted to a higher level so they may enter into the next higher realm.

If we find ourselves in the lowest realm of darkness and

horror, it is NOT because God threw us into that hideous realm. According to the research, there is no evidence that links hellish experiences with "bad" people. On the contrary, such states are encountered most often by ordinary people who lived ordinary lives. It is estimated the incidence of distressing NDEs ranges from 1%-15%. (Bonenfant, 2001.) Rommer (2000) concluded along with other NDE researchers' findings that as with pleasurable NDErs, virtually all distressing NDErs found their experience to have had a beneficial effect upon their lives. Bush (2002) reviewed the mystical literature of major religions and came to the same conclusion as Rommer: *Everyone has the potential to have a disturbing NDE.*

While not everyone who experiences a hellish NDE can be regarded as a bad person, a large number of people who report hellish NDEs describe themselves this way. Many of these people say, point blank, that selfish, materialistic, and/or God denying thoughts and behaviors on earth are what caused them to end up in hellish realms. Yet we have others who were clearly extremely bad people who reported having a beautiful, Light-filled experience.

Bottom line: we don't know the reason why distressing NDEs occur much less frequently than positive NDEs. We need further research in this area to answer this question.

However, this I do know: Because we are so loved, there will always be Divine assistance to those who find themselves in the lowest and darkest distressing realm. If they choose to accept that help, they will ascend to a higher, loving realm.

Howard Storm was a devout atheist all of his life. He suffered a perforated intestine, had a near-death experience and experienced that lowest realm where he endured great horror. The only thing he could think of doing was to think of the words of a Sunday School song his mother used to sing to him as a child. "*Jesus loves me this I know…*" Instantly, Jesus appeared to him and took him from that unspeakable realm of existence. Because Howard felt the love of Jesus for him, it transformed his life. He left his profession as a professor of art history at Northern Kentucky University, went to theological school and became an ordained minister. Such is the transforming power of the Creator's Love!

Each spiritual realm on the other side is progressively greater until one reaches the highest realm: the Heaven and Oneness of God. I can still remember during my life review the feeling of being sad that so many of us are living lives without any thought in preparation for the spiritual world. I had no previous knowledge about anything that I have so far discussed with you. Those revelations I was receiving during my experience were expanding my own spiritual consciousness, enriching and purifying it, thus allowing me to know with conviction that what I learned was of supreme value. It is what my Great Teacher revealed to me with the intent that I share this with others upon my return to the physical dimension. I promised that I would.

8

THE EGO –THE CAPTAIN
OF OUR SHIP

My Beloved,
To rely on Me means that you won't have to struggle with
uncertainty and fear. You will be at peace knowing I am
at your ship's helm steering your life in the direction of
safety.

I want to draw your attention to this aspect of our spiritual
development, because this was such an important lesson my
Great Teacher wanted me to learn and to share with others.
Prior to my experience, I did not know what the ego was
in relationship to our spiritual selves. I thought the word
"ego" meant that someone was full of themselves, egotis-
tical, stuck up. That was it. But I soon learned there was a
lot more to it than that!

You see, we try to understand spiritual wisdom with our
human intellect. It won't work. Truth must be spiritually
discerned through feeling rather than reason. Truth reveals
itself when it awakens the true inner self with peace and
love, for that is the Divine Presence, shining through us,
awakening that part of us that has been asleep for so long.

"Awaken, awaken, my sleepy children, walk with me; talk with me; be with me; I am your innermost teacher. Grasp your Divine consciousness; hold it, practice it, love it and share it."

Those words summarize the lengthy "conversation" I had with my Great Teacher concerning the relationship between transcending the ego-self and living from our real center of Divine Being.

The Light "downloaded" my lessons with lightning speed-all knowledge was being given simultaneously. Time was absent during my experience. I was given total knowledge from the beginning of "time" to infinity, and every word that ever was or will be communicated was made known to me. That is why it takes me "time" to write out some of my lessons in this way, for our physical reality is structured by time and you will have to take the time to read this in a linear time frame.

The lesson about the ego was a very important lesson for me to learn and to share with others. So here it goes. I hope you will pay very close attention to this lesson because when dealing with the ego, you will face challenges along the way from your ego-self, who believes it is the captain and the engine of your ship, running your life and navigating it according to its own authority. Our ego believes it to be our real self, and tenaciously holds onto this misidentification. It wants us to look outside of ourselves for validation from others for our worth as a person in order to make us feel good about ourselves. Through fear and negative thoughts, the ego is terrified of being destroyed, and will go to great lengths to deceive us by laying the blame on our unhappiness and suffering at the feet of others, or at the doorstep of life's circumstances. Ego will also try to steer us away from spiritual truths, by claiming its intelligence is far superior to this "woo-woo" stuff. That is why I say that this lesson is one to pay close attention to with an open mind. The ego has a very, very powerful voice; the soul has a soft and gentle voice. I urge you to listen to your gentle voice as we continue with this lesson, though it may be difficult.

As humans, we forgot who we are – our true nature, and as a result, we lost our awareness of our perfection and unity with God. Thus, we feel separated from God. Without that awareness, we have not developed our spiritual consciousness to the level of Divine Consciousness which always brings with it, peace, harmony, love, compassion, and mercy. Doubt, fear, or unbelief clogs our filters. If we cannot conceive that this Divine Power flows as through a channel into us, we have clogged the channel. To unclog it, we must eradicate our fear, hates, angers, prides, prejudices, inferiority feelings, and resentments, all of the various demons which inhibit harmony and to which the ego has been attached. We have to choose moment to moment whether we want to live in our own self- created torment, or live with the wondrous gift of a Divine life, unclouded by anxiety or fear.

I recall during my experience being shown an onion so I could understand this lesson of the ego and soul that my Great Teacher wanted me to comprehend. I guess God understands that sometimes I need visuals to simplify my understanding of something I didn't know about previously.

The onion is composed of removable layers of circular soft tissue that conceal the "heart" of the onion at its core. I understood the removing of each onion layer to be the removal of all the ego's false interpretations of who we truly are. As one peels each layer, one begins to go deeper into discovering things about oneself. Removing each layer one at a time, and thereby getting rid of the blocks that the ego's mind creates and instills in us, will eventually bring us to our core self, our true, Divine self.

At that core of our being, there is a place where we can know the experience of eternal peace. What stands between us and this peace is the unwillingness to acknowledge all our fears and sorrows as well as all the dark places in our hearts.

This is certainly not as easy as I make it sound. The struggle between the ego and the desire to be transformed towards becoming more spiritually present throughout our lives can be very difficult indeed. You only have to remember that life is a journey, and we are here to remember who we truly are and to express our true Light Nature from within us and into the world. That is the purpose of our lives! But it takes tremendous courage and discipline to lead such a life. If the physical body is acting purely as the instrument of the personality-self or ego, then willpower and conscience are controlled by the physical desires, which are apt to find a destructive outlet. Ego refuses to allow soul to function or reveal its truth. Soul, then, cannot make the proper connection with the physical body, which suffers as a result.

When we let ourselves and our lives be directed by love, it consumes our ego identity. Love begins to let go of everything our ego usually clings to – selfishness, fear, doubt, cruelty, competition, pride, arrogance, self-importance. But ego creates profound *attachment* – deep emotional and psychological attachment. So the last thing ego wants is to extinguish itself. It is the root of our problems that causes our pain and suffering.

When we become attached to anyone or anything, there is always the fear of loss that emerges from the ego self. The only true happiness and love lies within us as we get in touch with our true Divine Self, which is to be found within our own being. Light and love will emanate from us at all times when we are open to be a channel, each in our own way.

I am convinced that an individual gets what he really wants. He may desire things of the spirit –strength, love, new conditions, etc. If he doesn't get them, it is because he doesn't desire them as much as he does something else. It is that something else, not the circumstance, that creates a barrier for the soul to bring forth greater clarity to the mind of the individual.

Can we transcend the ego in one lifetime? I don't think so. We're here in earth school learning valuable lessons, and that takes an enormous amount of time to let go of the ego's identification as one's real self. It always waits in hiding, seeking out every moment to extinguish our Divine life. But one's happiness always means that one's Spirit is given the opportunity to conquer obstacles, to vanquish fear and doubt, to get on top of one's troubles. Happiness comes through activity of Spirit, never through inertia or brooding indifference. It means learning through our mistakes what and where happiness is and choosing it. Happiness has been given to us by the Divine Presence within us.

If we quietly sit on our butts waiting for some fairy godmother to wave her hand over us to change our lives for the better, then we will wait until our dying day and it won't happen. We need to get off our butts and take some action. We can rectify the mistakes we make, but if we never start, how can we move forward?

I am a gardener. I love to play in the dirt on my hands and knees and pull out the weeds that interfere with my plants' intended health and maturity. I continually check my rose bushes and prune out the dead and diseased stems and leaves. I also cut back some of the healthy stems in winter when the roses are dormant so that they will flourish more abundantly in the future. This pruning strengthens the rose bushes instead of weakening them. Often times while pruning, the thorns stab my arms or legs and I bleed.

As I reflect upon the challenge the roses offer me to help them to become healthier and happier, I am able to see that we too, need occasional pruning for complete growth. Yes, we will get to experience our own thorns and pain, and yes, we will bleed emotionally and physically. Pain can be the catalyst that prunes the unnessary emotions that ego wants to keep us tied to, distracting us from what is really important. Pain teaches us the lessons we either consciously or unconsciously refuse to learn.

If we don't prune away our stresses and what isn't healthy for us, pain will do it for us. But after the pruning, we're able to pause in the rose garden of our life and see what's important, meaningful, and essential for our growth and happiness. The intoxicating fragrance of the flowering of our best selves will reward us with great joy.

The object of my work is to inspire you to develop what will lead you to true happiness, which are the things of the Spirit. Whether it is due to laziness, fear, or both, we go to great lengths to put off the lessons we came here to learn. We find ourselves devoting most of our time and efforts to engaging in enormous distractions, both external and self-generated. When the ego is disturbed, all attention is focused externally, rather than toward, the focus of the soul. Even though we find ourselves in unpleasant or undesirable situations, by taking the time to explore and understand the meaning of these experiences by emotionally detaching from them, we can mature spiritually.

This can be a wonderful time of cleansing, letting go, and releasing the emotional baggage we have outgrown or no longer need. This baggage may be thoughts, perceptions, beliefs, attitudes, memories, and guilt feelings that once were useful to us, but are no longer needed. Once we cleanse our consciousness of these things, we make room for soul growth, allowing new insights, ideas, and intuitive thoughts that will emerge from our connection to the Divine Source we call God.

When the walls of the ego are lowered, we are the most receptive to the Divine whispers within us. Do not allow seeming human frailties to deter your forward motion toward your soul's growth. Remember that at the center of every human being is the Light, living through that human being. Each one moves forward as best he can according to his understanding.

The soul knows exactly what the individual is capable of accomplishing. Whenever it can, it flings him an inspiration, which, if he accepts it, may change him and his whole life completely. If he refuses to try, and flings it aside, he may lose his greatest opportunity to divert that course of action from the ego, and draw attention away from Spirit's call.

Spirit is such a God-sent blessing! It is here where love replaces sorrow, and where we can experience the peace and serenity that is our birthright. Love opens closed doors when one is willing to perceive what the Creator has intended for us to perceive. Each person's acceptance of this all-encompassing love brings the freedom to express his total Spiritual being upon the earth through his human personality.

Please don't get the impression that I am some saint who constantly lives my own life from an ego-free mindset. I, like everyone else on this planet, have moments when life throws a curve ball and I can feel myself falling through the cracks. My peace can be shattered in a blink of an eye when my ego demands that I follow along the path it wants me to take.

When my husband died, I was shattered. My mind was like a turbulent sea at the mercy of my emotions. My journey through grief seemed long and discouraging. I began to think I would never emerge from the broken heart of losing someone I loved so much. But I knew that God understood the weariness of my heart, and that when I was ready to rise above my ego's weariness, there would come without fail, a sustaining, refreshing grace to uphold this weary traveler on her journey.

I ask no one to pretend that they do not fear or to push their troubles from their heart, for in doing so, we keep ourselves at arm's length from life and healing. As long as we are participating in this physical world as human beings, it is important that we become *aware* of the ego's attempt at controlling and dominating us to the point where it will hurt us.

My point in talking about this is for all of us to remember that we are still in human form and we are learning the lessons that we came to earth to experience. Compassion is a lesson that our Great Teacher, the Light, would have us learn well. For one heart to extend compassion with a wordless, simple hug to someone whose heart is broken, is to unite the physical with the spiritual, bringing the two worlds together. The love of God, was being channeled through human beings whose compassionate hearts helped to ease my pain of grief, if only momentarily, with wordless hugs, or with caring words like, "I will pray for you." Compassionate friends acting from their hearts like that, rather than telling me how I should feel, is something I have never forgotten.

The pull towards a higher state of being is one that does not come easily to many people. The ego is aware of this, and right away, it wants to shine instead of Spirit. So many people decide to listen to that loud voice of the ego in order to stop the back and forth pull they feel. Should I listen to my ego or should I listen to my gentle inner voice within?

Again, reaching higher levels of spiritual growth does not mean transcending our human nature. As long as we are in human form, we should embrace our humanness, and the fullness of the human life, the pain and the sorrow as well as the joy. We need *balance* in order to experience our humanness with all our weaknesses while reaching for the heavens. Our humanness is the way we express our oneness with one another. To transcend that, and live as if one is above all that, is to miss the mark of being fully human.

Our mistakes, our fearful behavior, these are all part of the flow of human life as we journey our way toward a more enlightened existence. So, we should embrace every part of ourselves. But if there is an area that is not working for us and is causing misery, which is probably triggered by the ego, then we can choose to change it. It is an opportunity for growth, an opportunity for Spirit to work with us to guide us, replenish us, and prosper the purpose for which we are on earth.

I am spending some time on this lesson of the ego because it was such an important lesson my Great Teacher wanted me to learn and to share with others. What we humans deal with on a day-to-day basis is fear, worry, guilt, etc. This is *human nature* dominated by our ego-nature. We do the best we can under the circumstances. To expect us to suddenly transcend our humanness and be perfect is like closing our eyes and wishing for a million dollars to appear in front of us when we open our eyes. It's not going to happen. The best we can do is to become aware of our nature, whatever that is, and if it is not working for us, then we must change something. It's our choice.

I would highly recommend choosing to respond to life's challenges with love, gratitude, forgiveness, and compassion as the way to heal the ego of its desire to keep us as victims of shame, blame, mistrust, fear, betrayal, resentment, bitterness, sorrow, guilt, cynicism, and hatred. To value love above gain is life-transforming!

It takes a lot of work to undo those false beliefs about oneself, but it is not impossible to do. Recognize that it is ego that is damaging us in this way. The goal then is to slowly and gradually, calm that loud voice of the ego and reassure it that it doesn't have to dominate us in any way. When it starts to scream at us with those nasty negative emotions, we can speak gently to it and let it know that we are choosing to react to our outer circumstances with LOVE instead of fear, etc.

Everything and every moment can be chosen to be experienced in the precious energy of love. But again, it will take work. Ego wants to survive no matter what! You can see proof of that in our lives with all the negative energy at work within us. This battle goes back and forth until a person has clearly experienced the difference between the personality-ego-self and the soul. When the individual cooperates with the soul and begins working together with it, that's when they become infused with Divine Love and a new union arises.

I recommend trying to see ourselves with our true eyes, the eyes of our soul. If another person sees us in a bad way, that is NOT who we are. That is their problem, not ours! Their perception of us is based upon *their own ego nature*, not ours. For goodness' sake, we should let it go. We can calm that ego down by not giving it any power over us to accept, as truth, someone else's opinion of us.

The truth is, seen through the eyes of our soul, that we

are a beautiful, loving, precious, and worthy soul, endowed with the gifts of the Spirit and gifts of our human nature to be given in service to others. We can then hold our head erect and know this as the truth of our being. Then Spirit will reveal to us that beauty as we close the door to our ego-nature and its lies about us. We are LOVE – the very essence of the Light within us! So we should cultivate the habit of seeing ourselves radiating that Light, that beautiful, loving Light, and thus, healing our inner world.

While it is true that My Great Teacher allowed me to experience the greatest unconditional love in the entire universe, I was allowed to know the Divine nature of every man, woman and child. I want nothing more than for people to be able to trust what my Great Teacher wanted me to share with them. Trust with all your heart, with all your soul, with all your mind, in the Divine Presence of the Light who resides within you, for it is important to realize that which is Divine brings peace and, that which is not brings fear.

How can we know when we are expressing our soul consciousness or our personality ego-consciousness? Again, the ego is always thinking of self and what's in it for me. The soul thinks of service to others. The soul feels a connection to all things, while the personality-self feels separate. The personality-self acquires; the soul shares. The personality-self competes; the soul cooperates. The personality-self asserts self-will; the soul asserts Divine will. The personality-self often lacks direction while the soul has clear vision and purpose.

Those fleeting moments of kindness, love, inner peace, compassion, and forgiveness that we all have from time to time, are the experiences of our soul – our deepest essence of our higher self, of who we truly are. Our soul always tries to push us towards spiritual growth, to our next step as being its instrument of expression in the world. That moment when we touch the Center, the Divine essence of Being within us, we have contacted God. Rejoice! Rejoice!

9

WHAT LIFE REVIEWS HAVE
TO TEACH US

My Beloved,
Every word you speak has an effect on someone else. You
should always be aware that you have the opportunity
to speak kind words that will fall upon a secret place in
someone's heart to be valued and cherished.

When I had my life-review while in the presence of the
Light-God during my near-death-like experience, my
consciousness was elevated beyond my ego-consciousness.
Everything I was experiencing took on a clear, crystal clear
truthfulness, like a diamond casting its pure brilliance upon
my soul. Contrary to my religious beliefs, God was not
judging my earthly life; I was. I was ego-less at that point,
and because I had merged into Oneness with the Light, my
soul understood my Divine perfection even in the midst
of reviewing some negative events in my physical life. On
a much deeper level than the conscious mind, I was able
to see more clearly what the meaning and purpose of life
was – to be a reflection of the Light's Love into the world. I

was able to see how many times I failed to be that expression of love by choosing my lower self's ego's needs in lieu of the true self that is Divine.

If you get the impression that our life reviews can skip over the bad parts of our lives and reveal only the good parts, it doesn't work that way. Every thought, word, and deed that the soul experienced in human form was instantly exposed, laid bare before my eyes and the Light-God. Even though I felt great remorse for certain aspects of my life, the Light was loving me through my life review without condemning me or criticizing me in any way.

I realize that many traditional religions do not teach self-reflection and self-judgment when we die and face our Creator. They teach of a judgmental God who oversees the evaluation process of that soul, much like a criminal awaiting his/her verdict in a court of law. Now if I were the only person espousing a soul's own personal critique of their life during their life review, I would be, like many traditionally religious people profess, hesitant to believe what I am saying. However, nearly forty-plus years of research studies in the field of near-death experiences, have concluded from the thousands of individuals who have returned from the brink of death, that it is indeed the soul who judges its own life review. All the while, the Light is loving him/her unconditionally through that process. With so much research documentation before us, we can allow ourselves to be open-minded about this.

My Great Teacher taught me that we have two conflicting selves within us: our True Self and our false self, or our Higher and lower self. But I wasn't aware of that while going about my earthly existence. The choices I made were based mostly on everything negative. At times I was angry, worried, critical, foolish, unforgiving, and everything else that was at odds with my True Self. The unseen enemy, which I had been clutched by, was my ego.

There was one part during my life review experience when I had such guilt and remorse for the "sin" I committed in the past, (marrying an atheist.) Long story short, I was brainwashed by a priest who convinced me that God no longer loved me because of my failure to convert my soon-to-be husband atheist to the Catholic religion. This happened as a result of the church rules saying that engaged couples would first have to attend marriage counseling sessions with a priest before being married.

On our first appointment with the priest, we were expected to sign a paper stating our promise to raise any children we would have as Catholic. Ched refused, saying it was his belief that any children we would have should have the right to decide for themselves what religion, if any, they would want to pursue. He also admitted that he didn't believe in God. At that point, the priest terminated our session, telling us he would not marry us in the Catholic Church.

"*The sanctuary is not a place for atheists!*" he said in a domineering voice.

"*And you, young lady, I want to see you in my office Thursday evening at seven o'clock by yourself.*"

When I arrived at the priest's office that evening, I didn't know what to expect. I could tell however by his demeanor that he was not happy to see me. I felt scared but didn't know why.

"*Young lady, do you know why I want to see you?* He asked.

"No," I sheepishly replied.

"*Well, you have committed a mortal sin by intending to marry an atheist without converting him to Christianity, and specifically, to Catholicism, and you do not seem to have any remorse for this.*" His adamant booming voice made me feel like sinking into my chair. I felt ashamed. I felt confused. I felt guilty. I felt scared.

Why did I feel so bad, I wondered? No, this isn't right. I shouldn't feel this way, I thought.

After all, I was going to marry my soul-mate, a beautiful man whose moral and ethical values mirrored my own. I felt blessed that we had found one another. Surely God would forgive me if the priest was correct in saying that I had been committing a mortal sin by intentionally going ahead with marrying an atheist. After all, I had always felt that my relationship with God was extremely strong, ever since my childhood. The priest had to be wrong. Yes, that would be my defense.

For one month, three times a week, two-hour sessions, I argued that I was loved by God and that it wasn't my responsibility to convert my soon-to-be husband from atheism to Christianity. That was his own responsibility if he chose to do so. The priest on the other hand argued that I didn't know enough about Christian theology to be able to discern the truth of that situation. He told me it was his Christian responsibility to teach me right from wrong.

I did my very best to argue my position, and "if" I were sinning, certainly God would forgive me if I asked for forgiveness. After all, that is what I was led to believe about my faith. As long as one was sincere in admitting their "sin," whatever it was, God would forgive them. So I stood my ground firmly. I did not expect, however, that little by little, the priest would be able to annihilate my beliefs about a loving and forgiving God.

I was told that God could forgive a murderer, but not me. I was told never to pray again or go to church because I was so despicable that God no longer wanted a relationship with me.

The priest's final words to me as he pushed his chair from behind his thick, massive desk where he sat and showed me the door were,

"*You are the scum of the earth and unworthy of God's love or forgiveness.*"

By the end of the month, I was finally worn down by the priest's arguments and his scorn toward me. Something happens to a person when they become so emotionally beaten down that their own truth becomes nil. As a result, I took on, as absolute truth, the priest's perception of me, and I believed that I was going to end up in hell at the end of my life.

Ched and I did get married, but it was in his parents' Presbyterian Church.

For the next 16 years, I was devoid of the closeness I had felt with God, believing I was no longer loved. I could have become very angry with God, but I never had such feelings. I still loved God with all my heart. I just believed that I had sinned such a grave sin by marrying an atheist that I was doomed for hell. I couldn't pray or attend church because I felt despicable and believed that God wanted no relationship with me anymore. I had less than zero self-esteem.

Fast forward to my life-review 16 years later during my near-death-like experience. I saw that part of my life very clearly, and the associated guilt feelings I had suffered for those 16 years. I had lost all self-esteem because I trusted the priest's viewpoint over my own faith in a loving God.

It was only I who held the guilt to myself and who felt I had committed a sin. No, *I did not commit a sin to begin with* by intentionally marrying an atheist and refusing to convert him to Christianity according to the priest's agenda. But at that time in my young life, I believed that every word the priest told me was how God saw me. I felt I had to confess my "sin" and ask for forgiveness because that is what my religion taught me. But I soon learned that in God's eyes, I was always seen as the being of Light that God is, the beautiful inner soul, a purified Spirit of wholeness who sees through all human error, limitation, and frailty. *It was my own outer exterior self, my ego, that had blocked off my full understanding of a loving God!*

In retrospect, I can look back upon those 16 years with new vision. I can see that life experience as a gift that the priest unknowingly gave to me. Certainly not at the time was I able to have that wisdom, but following my experience I saw it very clearly. I saw how I was able to discover where I was vulnerable to be misled so that the vulnerability would be healed. In that way, I could become stronger in my connection to truth.

I receive many communications from individuals who are afraid of dying for fear that God will throw them away into a burning pit of fire. They believe that they have done something that is unforgivable, and that God doesn't love them, just as I felt so many years ago. Oh, how my heart breaks when they believe this. I think that is one of the reasons why I had my experience, so that I can relate to someone who has mistaken beliefs about God. I am a witness for them that God's Love is *unconditional*. I am able to be with them in a very intimate place to help them release their fear of a tyrannical, judgmental God. I know this is what God has called me to do. I will never tire of saying how much God loves every single one of us, no more, no less, than anyone else. Just imagine, no matter who we are or what we have done, we are loved as much as a saint! Please don't wait until you have your own life review to discover this truth! Live with that truth **now**, so that your life will be all that God desires for you. Don't waste one more moment thinking that you are unworthy of God's love. **It's just not true!**

I was able to understand the role of my ego-false self so that I wouldn't feel ashamed or guilty over my foolishness when I returned once more to my physical consciousness. If I make mistakes, which I do, it is just a matter of recognizing who did it. My ego, the false self, was the one who did it, not my real spiritual, or Divine Self. Once recognized, it is easier to get back on the right path again by forgiving myself or others so that I can continue to live in love, peace, and harmony. To know beyond all doubt that the Divine Presence is the reality of our being, is to give it dominion over our lives, and to rely more and more on Divinity unfolding and revealing Itself as us.

During my life-review, placed deep into my awareness was the understanding that God recognizes that our earthly consciousness ruled by our egos, have filters that make us incapable of always selecting the right choices that a fully developed spiritual consciousness would make. Further, as humans, we may realize we have been born into this world with a soul, but we do not have the full understanding of it. No more than a young child understands intellectual concepts that surpass his level of comprehension. We have not become aware that we are innately connected to the Power Source that ceaselessly flows within us to lead the way that takes our soul to the truth of God.

When my Great Teacher, the Light, through Divine Grace, took my Spirit-self into the heart of God while my physical body was delivering a eulogy, something very profound happened to me. I remember that the very first thought I had, as soon as I had lifted out of my body, was,

"Oh my God, that was all an illusion that I just left. I am now in the REAL reality with God! I am HOME!"

An illusion? What do I mean? Trust me, that knowledge was factual. A great truth was revealed to me, even though I cannot explain the physics of it so your physical brain can comprehend this. I think this is probably the hardest thing to explain to someone who views our human reality as absolute reality, and who believes with certainty that it is not an illusion we are living.

"*What an absurd idea*," some will say, but I will do my best to explain according to what my Great Teacher, the Light, taught me.

The illusion we humans live in is like a dream. It is a partial reality that is only a small part of the complete awareness that our true nature is, as individualization's of Infinite Divine Consciousness. I understood that, outside of God, there is no other reality; **only God is real.** That is why I understood that the earthly dimension I had just transcended was not real as I had always understood it to be. It was an immense revelation, as if a dense outer covering of my mind had become porous to the rays of the Light enabling me to comprehend that truth.

I understood that the illusions that binds us to the earth are the temporal conditions of the flesh. The more we identify with them, the more intense is the illusion, thus creating its limitations which are difficult to surmount.

My Great Teacher, whose cherished unconditional love was overseeing my life-review with me, reminded me that I had been living in the illusionary realm of appearances and fulfilling my self-serving desires brought on through living by the whims and dictates of the lower self. The Light was perceiving me not as some sinful monster who needed to be sent to hell, but instead, as a small child who had not yet learned the lessons that earth school wanted me to learn. I had not yet developed my soul consciousness to look into the heart of every man to see the Light, the presence of God within everyone.

To accelerate my learning, the Light simply allowed me to see my Divine self which, in turn, substantially nourished the regeneration of my soul as I learned the meaning and purpose of my life, and in fact, of all of our lives.

Once again, God loves us unconditionally, no strings attached. There is no need to beat ourselves up for our mistakes with a lot of guilt feelings or approach death with fear that God will punish us. We are learning our lessons while we are here on earth. The healing of the wounds of our past is to be found in forgiving ourselves, and in God's Love for us. I want with all my heart for people to simply accept that precious Love with the vivid awareness that God's continuous Presence with us is a Sacred gift, no matter who we are, or what we have done.

We are here on earth to experience many opportunities to learn what our soul wants us to learn. It may be any number of spiritual qualities, such as compassion, patience, service, or love. No matter what age we are, we are like children, learning our life's lessons and making mistakes in the process. When we went to school and made mistakes on our tests, did we suffer needlessly from guilt feelings? Probably not. We were given the correct answers and we learned from those mistakes. We moved on to our next lessons. The Light sees us as children making mistakes while learning our lessons. It would be a cruel God who would punish us in ways that would cause us to back away from that tender, Sacred Love, and resort to feeling unworthy of it.

My life review was an outstanding lesson that catapulted my spiritual growth to new heights of consciousness, because

I began to understand myself better, and understand my fellow human beings as well. With this understanding comes love, and responsibility, a responsibility to God, self, and others. I now understand that I have created every experience in my life, the positive and the negative ones, for my benefit and for my learning. Knowing my true worth, my Divine value, knowing life as oneness with all living creatures, is to know and feel the great joy of the Eternal One.

If I have one message to shout from the rooftops to all who can hear me, I would say, *"Don't wait until you die to have your life review. Live your life review NOW!"* Your lifetime mission on earth is to know yourself as thoroughly as you can, and to love yourself and others without qualification. Treasure the knowledge of your Divine Self above all other knowledge. It is your personal truth. Your selfhood is your uniqueness, your abilities, your justification for being. It is the One Divine Power expressing Itself through our beings on the human level.

We spend so much precious time learning things which in the end, are not really that important. What we acquire by learning is useful to the intellect, stored in the cells of our brains, and dies with our physical bodies. Only what we experience, perceive intuitively, and moves our spirit within; that alone is what we will take with us. How much did we experience love, compassion, forgiveness, and service to others?

We may desire to acquire *spiritual* knowledge and to realize truth, but we have to grow accustomed to this wisdom as our mind adjusts to receive it. Simply being interested in realizing spiritual wisdom is not enough to actualize it. The way to discovering truth is the result of the soul preparing us well. Otherwise, the ego curtails our progress with preconceived ideas and prejudices, and that's when we usually give up the pursuit.

We can't expect others to reveal the whole truth to us; whatever is revealed is the result of our own sincere desire, and of our own ability to receive it.

I do not pretend to tell you anything new, merely to show you how to go about acquiring truth for yourself. If the ray of Light which I can guide you to will provide you with an opportunity for spiritual growth, I will be delighted, but I can only point the way. Spiritual wisdom is yours when you have evolved your soul and its powers sufficiently to recognize wisdom when you see it face to face. Then you will become sensitive to the rays of Light that will clear away the shadows, and fill the dark places with illumination, allowing you to see a true picture of life from a higher vantage point.

Divine Love chose to express itself as you. Keep in your heart, like a luminous jewel, the presence of the Light, and share this Divine Presence with those you come in contact with. Continue to work to peel off false judgments and pre-conceived ideas of how life ought to be, and accede to the Source in every situation, so that a new idea of how life can be may fill your mind. Each hour, each day, each week, let the love of God within your life increase, allowing nothing to bind or limit your Spirit. You see, it's not what we say or believe, it's what we DO while we are living in the here and now that determines what happens to us after we cross over to the next realm.

Please be aware that our life-reviews at the end of our physical deaths reveal every thought, word, and deed that we have experienced during our entire lives. It's a feeling as if we are *actually reliving* those moments. We get to feel what it was like for someone we manipulated, bullied, argued with, hurt, and so on. Actually feeling what the other person felt like when we were unloving towards them is not pleasant, believe me. On the other hand, it is a wonderful feeling to experience what someone felt like when we offered that person our love, support, forgiveness!

Everything created comes from God. Look everywhere to see the Divine Nature in all things. As our awareness of it springs forth, we then feel love and peace. It's easy to see the beauty of the Divine in many things, but harder to spot it in places or in people who we are critical of.

When we judge others in a negative way, we won't feel the peace and love that comes with seeing that person or situation endowed with the Divine Nature that is of God. We need to stretch the limits of our being and change our thoughts at that moment. In choosing to see everything around us with having the Spirit of the Divine pulsing in the heart of all things, we will soar on enlightened wings of love and peace once again.

Our lives right now are the lessons we are learning. We should make use of every opportunity to advance our soul's journey to the Light, NOW while there is still time. You see, time is like a river. We cannot touch the water twice, because the flow that has passed will never pass again.

The best way of raising our spiritual vibration is by unselfish service to others and being motivated to touch hearts by acting from a base of LOVE and forgiveness. So live your life review NOW, so that this very moment is touched by your Divine Nature. Then when you come to the end of your earthly life and return to the Light, your life review will be a virtuous one and you will have few regrets.

10

Q & A'S

My Beloved,
Ask how best you can serve and I will show you the way.

The following discussion is a compilation of questions that some folks have emailed me and the manner in which I addressed them.

Q. Nancy, how can I know for sure that God and an afterlife exist? I am a scientist and I need proof.

A. I can assure you there is another dimension or realm far greater than this earthly one. Our left brains, ego, and especially science demands "proof." But in my opinion, science will never be able to put God under the microscope and understand the way He works. Think of it this way: Science has discovered all the elements that make up a human body. We know how much potassium, magnesium, calcium, hydrogen, etc. that constitute a physical body. If you put all those elements into a big vat, you could then say that science has discovered what makes up a human being, right? But what about that one element that science cannot duplicate?

Life! It's that invisible "stuff" that cannot be measured, or reproduced. It escapes our scientific understanding. That's the God-part, that mysterious gift that we have been given.

There are so many theories about the near-death experience, but no one will ever, in my opinion, be able to "extract" that same invisible "stuff" about the nature of God, who is, in my opinion, the Source of these experiences, just as *life* is that part that science can't reproduce by putting all the elements of the human body together. It's just our ego's human nature and our need to understand everything before we can trust its validity. But God is so much more than our finite minds can understand. It's so easy for me because I was on the other side of the veil and I saw and heard with my own supernatural eyes and ears. That was my own proof. I have great compassion for those who weren't on the other side to know from direct experience and who are struggling with questions that seem to have no answers.

My favorite Biblical passage is this one: "*You believe because you have seen, but blessed are those who haven't seen and yet believe.*" There is so much to be said about developing our faith to carry us through this journey of life, because we will always have unanswered questions about the mystery of life. We must be willing to realize that the great mystery cannot be understood by the mind. It is our ego that is always pushing us to comprehend the great unknown in terms that will satisfy it. But to truly know the mystery, we need to be willing to live in a state of unknowing, where the ego is no longer creating the barrier to the discovery of who we are beyond the ego – the True Self.

Faith is revering what we cannot understand, without demanding that science has to prove it. At the deepest level, our hearts believe what our minds cannot explain. This kind of faith moves us beyond the senses into the mystical, the process of growing into the Divine Presence who reveals truths the eye cannot see. We awaken, from the old patterns of habits and conditioned thinking, into new ways that make space for the Divine life to come through.

As for trusting the validity of the existence of life after death, I think the more you delve into the near-death experience research data, the easier you will find it to trust that life after death exists. With over forty years of research, and having studied thousands of experiencers, it is unlikely that so many people would be fabricating such stories. Jeffrey Long, M.D., radiation oncologist and New York Times best-selling author of the book, *Evidence of the Afterlife: The Science of Near-Death Experiences*, hosts a website (www.nderf.org) which has become the largest near-death experience research database in the world. He estimates that 774 cases of near-death experiences occur every day. A thorough examination of the research data that has been made available to the general public should help to convince you of the legitimacy of life after death.

Q. You said at one point during your experience that you saw everyone. Did you see me?

A. Yes, I did, although during the experience, I saw everyone simultaneously. Time and space were absent. Upon my return to the physical dimension, time and space re-appeared and with that, can you imagine the amount of "time" it would take to remember the actual face of someone I saw during my experience? There would be no way to remember it all. It is impossible for people to understand the concept of timelessness and everything happening simultaneously. So I really can't help your left brain to comprehend this. It is equally difficult to understand the concept of oneness, which is what I experienced when I "saw" every person on the face of the earth. I had transcended any sense of being separate. We were all one. Every person on the face of the earth was being loved the same as everyone else, and that was with a love unimaginable. That is why I am so passionate about helping others not to judge themselves unworthy of the Creator's love, no matter who they are or what they have done. All are loved equally – the saint and sinner alike. I experienced that Divine, unconditional Love for **you** as well as for myself.

Q. How long must I wait to get an answer from God to know what I am supposed to be doing? I get so impatient.

A. Everything is on a Spiritual timetable and that includes understanding and realizing your destiny. When the time is right, it will happen. Sometimes I get impatient myself because I want to do more and more for the Light-God. So I understand where you are coming from. As long as your heart is welcoming the Spirit that moves in and through you, it will come to fruition. Patience, my friend, is a virtue. Granted, it's not easy, though. It's the journey we are on. It will happen though!

Do you meditate or listen quietly to that still, small voice within? That is the best way to be guided in your life. We need to turn off the left brain and listen without ego's voice getting in the way. I am not suggesting that we have to get rid of the ego and that it must die. Some choices the ego makes become stepping stones on our journey to discover ourselves. However, sometimes it's just the wrong tool for the job. Spiritually, we need to go to that soft, quiet place where our Source can bring us the guidance we seek.

Prayer, meditation, and just being still are the best ways to get in touch with our Spiritual selves. Sometimes we need to remind ourselves that maybe we are doing what we are supposed to be doing.

Many of us try too hard to find our answers, and that's when we will never find them. The idea is to let go of that ego. Let go completely and surrender to the great unknown. The point at which your heart is open so wide, in perfect stillness, is a place where the great unknown can surface. Meditation and prayer are wonderful tools as long as you renounce ego's hard-shell control over you. This takes a lot of work, but it can be done.

Q. Do you believe in synchronicities?

A. I do believe in synchronicities. When the time is right for the gift to appear, things move into place as if by magic. Something more is at work in our universe than mere physical laws of cause and effect. When synchronicities occur, it's like stepping into the universal flow, which opens our minds to the possibility of connecting with Spirit. They happen all around us, often preparing the way for our next opportunity, whether it is intended to help us or to help someone else. The key is to acknowledge the timing of these events and to see their purpose. That's when we grow and move past the ordinary into the "extraordinary." Spirit works this way for people to learn, share and grow spiritually. The more we honor them and acknowledge them, the more often they will appear for us. It's the universe's way of thanking us for being open and receptive to the opportunities that will benefit us in some way.

Q. I am skeptical about these types of experiences. I believe there must be a logical explanation for them.

A. I was once on a television talk show which presented a balanced guest list including a true-blue skeptic. He made a hard case for his beliefs and it was very hard to convince him otherwise. I believe if someone is a skeptic, no amount of explaining will suffice until that skeptic's ego allows him to open his mind more, at least to consider the *possibility* that he may be incorrect in his beliefs. Unless one has had this profound experience, it sounds "wacko!" But for those having it, it is more REAL than reality itself. The proof of the experience, although it is subjective, is the transforming power that occurs in the individuals having the experience. The changes are dramatic. People change careers; they love more deeply; they forgive others; they become more spiritual.

What do you think causes such dramatic changes in someone's life? Neurons misfiring in the brain? Hallucinations? Lack of oxygen to the brain? Why is there a **spiritual** component to the experiences? Why did Howard Storm, an acquaintance of mine, who was a university professor of art and a devout atheist, suddenly change careers following his near-death experience and become an ordained minister? Why does someone like me who was every bit as ordinary as your next-door neighbor suddenly have this transcendent life-changing experience? Why is my entire life devoted to serving God and helping others when I wasn't this way prior to my experience? Why? Why? Why? Good questions, but I still believe these experiences are not the result of brain chemistry, but originate from a loving Higher Power who is transforming souls one at a time, every day in order to bring a message of **love** to humanity. With over 774 near-death experiences per day according to Dr. Jeffrey Long, it may suggest that we are having a profound shift in universal consciousness. This doesn't even include those individuals who had near-death-like, spiritually transformative experiences who weren't close to death, or suffering serious illness, or physical trauma. Those figures would then soar! Something very profound is happening to millions of people throughout the entire world, and it is a *spiritual* happening.

Q. I would like to draw closer to God, but I don't know how.

A. To answer your question about becoming closer to God, first let me address the meditation issue, which is an excellent way to draw closer to God. At first, meditation is very hard because the ego is constantly trying to pull you away from it by "thinking" too much. Those disruptive thoughts get in the way. But that's very normal for a beginner trying to meditate. With constant practice, however, it gets easier. Are you familiar with the relaxation technique where you begin concentrating only on one part of your body, such as your toes, and gradually relaxing all parts of the body?

I like to lie down when I meditate, while others prefer to sit. With your eyes closed, you focus your attention only on your toes, and mentally, you tell your toes to relax. Continue to focus only on your toes, repeating your instruction to your toes to relax. Soon you should feel the muscles begin to relax. If they don't, keep instructing the toes to relax until you feel a sense of release. Once you relax your toes, then move up to your ankles and do the same. Continue to move up your entire body, instructing each muscle part to relax and release any and all tension in those muscles. It is common to feel such peace when you reach the top of your head that sometimes you might just fall asleep! You may think, "Duh! I 'failed' in my attempt that time to meditate.

Oh well. Perhaps you needed the short nap more than you needed to meditate that time, and that's okay; there's always another time.

This process helps quiet the busy ego mind, because you can't hold two thoughts in your mind at the same time. I would suggest that you first begin your meditation in this manner. Don't go any further with it. Just get used to this practice of stilling your ego mind so that your muscles begin to have cell memory as you instruct them to be at peace every time you want to connect with the meditative process. Eventually, you can move on to go deeper, where you can begin to receive guidance from your inner Source.

When I get to that completely relaxed state, I give myself mental instructions to visualize a scene so that I can begin to feel as if I am going there in my mind. Whatever scene appeals to you, then create that in your mind. For me, it is always nature. In my mind, I take a walk in the woods and I visualize what every detail I encounter during my walk looks and feels like. I "see" the pebbles in the dirt path I am walking on; I catch a glimpse of a bird in a tree. I notice what color the bird is. I see what type of beak it has, either long, or short, thin or stout. I look closely at its feathers and touch them to "feel" the softness underneath my fingertips. I let myself continue to walk in the woods, allowing whatever I see along my path to present itself to me. Always, I continue to feel relaxed. If, at any time, I sense any tension in any part of my body, I go back to that muscle and tell it to completely relax as if a helium balloon is lifting tension out of my body and floating it up, up, and away.

The journey through the woods is very enjoyable. I always tell myself to go to the clearing in the woods where the sunlight is shining more brightly. I envision that my Great Teacher, the Light-God, is waiting for me by a stream where two large boulders are perched beside that stream. My Great Teacher is sitting on one, and the other is reserved just for me. As I walk closer, the sparkling rays of golden light begin to fill every particle of my being with love. As this Divine Love fills my heart, and mind, every atom, every cell of my body feels purified.

Then I sit on the rock and ask my Great Teacher for guidance. If I have a question, I ask the question and ask to be guided in my understanding. At that point, I just allow whatever happens to present itself to me. I just go with the flow. It may be thoughts that surface; it may be another scene that appears that will help me understand something, it may be my Great Teacher who speaks to me. I just allow whatever happens without any further participation on my part. If I don't understand something, or want another question answered, I ask again.

When I am finished meditating, I usually end my visit by thanking my Great Teacher for being present with me and helping me with whatever wisdom or guidance I was seeking. I usually hug Him before leaving, and then I walk home through the woods feeling intense gratitude, humility and love. Slowly, I bring my mental attention to my physical body, lying down, and slowly open my eyes. Meditation is over.

Sometimes all I desire is simply to be present with the Light-God during meditation, period! I would suggest that you do this initially. Get used to the Holy Presence first without wanting anything more. Eventually, you can move on to requesting guidance. The more you practice this, the easier it will become. It may be weeks or even months before you can successfully meditate. Ego is stubborn and very persuasive. But it is worth the effort to transcend it so you can experience a deepening experience of the Divine

Presence within. Meditation is a good way to go deeper into the realm of Spirit, as is prayer.

Q. How can you be sure that God will never abandon me because of something bad I have done?

A. Believe with your whole heart that God loves you more than we can comprehend, no matter who you are or what you have done. I learned that when we have that kind of faith, it is the faith that moves mountains, and nothing is impossible. For most people, the ego gets in the way and jeopardizes this gift of faith. I know that God desires that we have this kind of unshakable faith because God wants all of our longing and love to be centered upon Him – not ourselves, as is our ego's desire. I sympathize with those who are so adamant that reality is only based on what our five senses can prove. It is hard to put that aside and trust in something unseen. In many ways, it is true that we must become like a small child with that kind of trust in the Holy One. It was a promise from the Light to me during my experience that God is always with us and will never leave us for any reason– never! Place your hand in God's Hand and He will superglue your hand to His for eternity.

Q. How can I trust and believe that what you say is true?

A. I can tell you this: No one has absolute truth to teach you. We all have bits and pieces of truth. You will only find truth within you from the Source that is present within. You should never accept anything someone tells you just for the sake of it. Always, you must go within and let your inner Voice reveal the truth. One hint is that if the information is loving and you feel inner peace with it, your inner Voice will respond with a feeling of love and peace; there will be no conflict. "Something" will resonate deep within you that it is true. Ego, however, will step in and try to pull you away quickly. I suspect that is why you are being pulled in two directions at the same time. Ego must be quieted before peace and truth will become recognized.

There are stages to our spiritual development. First comes the decision to follow this path toward our true inner life. Then we begin asking a lot of questions about the purpose of life; we are confused and we want all the answers. We are compelled to find teachers, read books, and attend workshops to help us to find that guidance. We begin to re-evaluate things.

As Henry David Thoreau once said, "*It's not what you look at that matters, it's what you see.*" As we put our trust in the Divine Presence within to guide us, we begin to see through a new set of eyes to discover the beauty that is within. Be willing to see from the love and wisdom and integrity that springs forth from within.

The second stage is more difficult and challenging because you will feel the pull of the ego and your spiritual nature being at odds with one another. I would encourage you to keep on the path, no matter how difficult it may be. Your life experiences will be your best teachers. After all, we came here for those difficult experiences in order to develop our spiritual nature.

The last stage in your spiritual development may never be attained, because it is rare to reach this level of development within one's lifetime. But should you find yourself here, it is where you will feel as if you have been reborn. Everything will look very different from when you first started this spiritual journey. It will be a state of grace when ego has been transcended, and you, as your real self, will resemble and reveal the character of the Spirit of the Divine.

I know you probably want to go from the first stage to

the last and skip all the ones in between. Keep trusting your heart no matter what happens. It will lead you to where you need to go, and in the timeframe that is needed. Always keep trusting in the Source of your truth within. The more you lean on the Divine Presence within, the more will be revealed to you.

I can only *lead you to the doorstep*, but I can't push you inside God's Heart of Truth. That is a journey you must make all by yourself and in your own time. Again, meditation and prayer help. It's quieting the ego's need to analyze everything. I know that's hard, and I don't mean to belittle that. Gosh, I know how analytical thinking is so prevalent in our lives. Use that type of thinking where it is needed, in our jobs, healthcare, research, safety, etc. But when coming to the Divine Presence within, simply trust and in faith, believe. That inner Presence will teach you by the intuitive part of yourself giving you signs in your heart. Does the wisdom "feel" right? Does the wisdom bring you peace? Does the wisdom bring you a sense of love? **Does the wisdom draw you closer to God?** All those signs come from the Light within, whispering in your heart to trust Divine Wisdom and not the wisdom of men.

Ego will then try to convince you not to feel those things. Ego will try to convince you to listen to its voice. Ego wants to be "right." Ego wants to survive in spite of everything and to be superior. Ego wants to pull us away from God by shouting its voice loudly at us to listen to **it** instead of the soft, inner voice of our Beloved. The Divine Voice within will prove itself authentic because we won't have any more questions. We will have our answers. Ego's loud voice won't bother us anymore because we are resting in Divine Love and Truth, and nothing can draw us away from that reality. The trick is to recognize ego's voice when it speaks and then remind ego that you are choosing to go within and find refuge within the Peace of God. Then, when ego's voice has been quieted, be with God. Ask anything, and wait for the answer to stir within your heart. It takes practice, so don't rush the process.

Q. I have heard that we are co-creators with God. Please explain.

A. Yes, we co-create with the Creator of the Universe in the following manner: We choose to be instruments or vessels of Divine Love, Grace, Healing, and other great works by giving ourselves permission to open ourselves to receive the power from Spirit to manifest our great works in this materialistic world. By our own power, we are weak, but with Divine Power in and through us, we are strong! When we choose the desire to serve the Creator and others, then it is our desire to be subject to the ways in which we are called to do this great work.

Look at it this way: I never had a desire to write books, for goodness sake, never in a million years did I ever desire such a thing! Then one day, wham, I'm suddenly with the Light-God in Heaven, where I was "told" to speak and write. You could say I was "ordered" to do this work. But during my experience, before I could reply to this directive, I was told very specifically not to answer until I knew the cost that would be involved to me personally. It would be an act of my freewill whether I wanted to proceed with this "calling."

That's when I had my life preview and saw what my work for the Light would entail. I saw visions of both the positive and negative aspects of the calling I was being given. The best decision of my life was when I promised to fulfill this calling no matter what I had to go through. I chose to do this because of the tremendous love I was feeling for God at that time, and because I wanted to return a gift of love in service to others in return for the gift of love I was being given at that time.

So in the process of becoming an instrument for the Light-God, I am also co-creating with God to bring the intended purpose to fruition. I can't write! That's right, I can't write. It took me years of frustration sitting at my computer trying to figure out what I was supposed to write. When I had reached the point where my ego was shut down and the only thing left was God, that's when things blossomed. The words poured out of me, into the computer and into book form. I had co-created with God to bring that wonderful book, *Hear His Voice* and four others into physical manifestation. At any time, I could have called it quits and stopped. But I didn't. God had poured so much Love into me while I was writing that I felt I had traveled back to Heaven again. How could I not write with so joyful a feeling as that? How could I not be a willing vessel when God was working so joyfully *with me* like that?

Pierre Teilhard de Chardin, a French philosopher and Jesuit priest, once said that *"Joy is the infallible sign of the Presence of God."*

Let me give you another example of how I became a co-creator with God for another book I had written. This is a true story, honest! After my first book, *Hear His Voice*, was published, I thought I was finished writing books. I had no plans to continue writing, because I had honored my promise to God to write that first book. So I thought I was off the hook, so to speak, from writing any further. But God had something else planned for me.

At that time, my husband was having kidney dialysis treatments due to end-stage renal failure. I drove him to his dialysis center three times a week and waited for him in the waiting room for the five- hour-long dialysis treatments. We lived quite a distance from the dialysis center, so it was easier for me to remain there instead of driving home again, then driving back to the center to pick my husband up and then drive back home again.

Waiting for that length of time began to wear on me. There were other elderly women also waiting for their husbands, and they all couldn't hear very well. They turned the television on what seemed to me to be full blast to watch CNN News. Most near-death experiencers will tell you that once we return to physical consciousness, we abhor loud noises, and we have difficulty watching television or movies which depict any form of violence or hurtful actions toward other human beings. I rarely watch the news for that reason. So for me, sitting for five hours in the dialysis waiting room with loud noise emanating from the television, and trying not to focus on the news being presented, was becoming more than I could endure.

I managed to tolerate it for one year, but after that, I knew I had to change something. I was not about to tell ten elderly women that they couldn't watch the news anymore or that the volume would have to be turned way down for my sake, resulting in them not being able to hear their news program. No, I had another plan in mind. I learned that there was a local library in the vicinity, so as soon as my husband was hooked up to his dialysis machine, I left the building and went there.

Once at the library, I went to the sound-proof sitting room reserved for people who don't wish to be disturbed for any reason. It was so calming, the outer layers of my mind and emotions were laid aside. I rested in the innermost place of stillness and found myself thinking of the Light-God.

Deeper and deeper my love was being felt, until it entered

the union stage with God. This is quite natural for me to reach this level of intimacy with God. The awareness that I am able to feel of the Eternal One dwelling in me, to such a degree that it permeates my whole being, is beyond what I am able to speak or write about.

Silently, I talked with God. I filled every particle of my being with God's breath. Suffice it to say, I was humbled by the intense feelings of gratitude for my ongoing relationship with God, and soft tears began to flow from my hazel eyes. I had nothing to wipe the joyful tears away, so I just let them flow. My back was turned to others in the room, so I was basically unnoticed.

I was having a silent "conversation" with God in my mind, talking about my dedication to fulfilling the calling I was given during my encounter with the Light-God while delivering a eulogy in 1979. Not one day has gone by since that time when I haven't re-dedicated myself to loving service. That spiritually transformative experience of the inner God, has created an understanding of real love that the inner chamber of my heart can never forget. This ineffable love calls me to spend daily moments with the Source of my being. So, for the most part, my time spent with the One Most High in the library was my time to withdraw from the tumult of the outer world, and to feel the bright flame of the Holy Spirit in my heart. Apparently, my expanding consciousness of God allowed me to hear the Light's Voice within my heart.

Breaking the silence of my inner world, suddenly, a beautiful thought crossed my mind which shocked me. It appeared without my attention on anything other than what I had been talking to God about. The thought was unrelated to anything in my mind at the time. As soon as the thought passed, I could not remember what it was. I only knew that it didn't come from my own thought process.

"*Oh well,*" I thought, as I resumed, once again, my conversation with God. But soon, another beautiful thought entered my mind. Again, I couldn't remember it afterwards. Again and again this happened while I was spending time in communion with God in that sound-proof room in the public library.

Each time I went to the library, I centered myself in the same way, allowing my Spirit-self to commune with God. I was not asking God for anything at all; I was just engaged in being in love with God. Those moments are so precious to me that I find myself throughout each and every day drawing near to the Divine Presence within me. Once again, while my thoughts were focused upon letting God know how much I loved God, how grateful I was for everything in my life, etc., more beautiful thoughts passed through my mind. By this time, I was getting a bit used to the idea that these thoughts were coming from a Source other than my own mind. I wanted to remember those thoughts, but I always forgot them immediately after they passed through my mind.

Weeks went by, and each time I went to the library, the same thing happened to me. Since I could not recall the thoughts, I decided to bring a notebook with me the next time so I could quickly jot them down. My intent was simply to save them for my own personal use.

Several months later, I found that notebook at home with the beautiful messages that I had jotted down. When I began to read them, I was shocked! They were so beautifully written! I knew I had not written them from my own mind. The messages were beyond what my tiny, human mind can manifest on its own. Upon reflection on how those messages came to be, I discerned that it was Spirit whispering the words in my ear and the only thing I had to do was to write them down.

Now, what to do with them, I wondered. I prayed. I elevated my Spirit-self to union with the Holy One and asked if I was supposed to share those beautiful messages with the world, and if so, I prayed that the reader would be assured of the authenticity of the messages as coming from the Divine Source and not from me. I felt that I was only the pencil in God's Hand. The true author of those messages was God.

I would like to share with you a gift I received following my near-death-like experience. When I want guidance from God, I hold a closed Bible over my heart and close my eyes. After I have entered a communion relationship with God through deep, sincere prayer, I ask God to lead me to a passage that will speak to my heart about my concern or need. With my eyes still closed, I move my index finger back and forth approximately two inches above the closed Bible. When I see a white light in the corner of my left eye, I immediately poke my finger into the closed pages of the Bible and I open my eyes and begin reading the passages on the opened pages. Always, a specific answer to my prayer appears. Always!

As you recall, I asked God during my prayer to confirm that all the messages came directly from the heart of God and not from the mind of this author, Nancy Clark. I was led to the following passage using the technique just described.

John 14:10 *"The words I say are not my own but are from my Father who lives in me. And he does his work through me. Just believe it-that I am in the Father and the Father is in me."*

Need I say more? **As God is my witness, what I have stated is the truth!**

I am sure that there will be individuals who cannot believe what I just said. It sounds too good to be true. Perhaps they will want to call me a liar, a deceitful person, so their own egos can disengage themselves from accepting this truth. But if you can wrap your head around what I am telling you, then you will have to come to the spiritual conclusion that this is a so-called "miracle" brought forth from the Creator. On my own, I would never be able to open a Bible with my eyes closed and read a passage that is so interrelated to the prayer I was just speaking of. This happens every time I do this technique! Ask a statistician what the odds of having a passage appear like that – so specific to a question I am asking God at that time. I could never, ever fabricate this to deceive anyone. I love God too much to be disloyal like that to God and to others.

Those messages were then published in my book, *My Beloved: Messages from God's Heart to Your Heart*, which also became a national award-winning book.

So many people contacted me after reading that book telling me they were dealing with something that was bothering them, and they opened my book randomly, and it was as if God had led them to a specific message they needed to hear at that time. It became a real blessing for so many people. That is why these messages must be shared in any way that I am able to share them. They must be kept alive to let people know how much God loves each and every one of us unconditionally.

I have included some of those messages from my book, *My Beloved*, in this book. They appear at the bottom of each chapter page.

With every book I wrote after that first book, including this book, I became aware that God was nudging me to continue writing. I thought I had finished my work after *Hear His Voice* was written, but oh no, God wasn't finished working with me yet. So I continue to keep my promise to write, and I will until I get the word, from the True Author of all my books, that it has come to an end. But I do believe this will be my last book as my golden years are winding down, seemingly faster every day.

We are co-creators with God in the sense that as we raise our spiritual energy or vibration when we transcend the ego, we are in direct contact with the Divine. *"As a man thinketh, so he is."* Our thoughts create our reality. Those words were words I understood completely during my experience. If we believe with complete faith that Spirit will bring us our intended good, and if we raise our faith to the level where our thoughts are purely and positively and unquestionably positive and loving, then we are in sync with the energy of the Divine. We will then, *together*, bring about the intended good **if** what we desire is our destiny.

Remember, we signed up for this job here on earth. Our souls know what we are supposed to do and what we are supposed to learn. Our egos don't remember. Every experience gives us that opportunity to grow in the manner we are intended and what we signed up for. Spirit is helping us to learn what we came here to learn. Spirit knows what the best experiences will be for us. Even if they are tragic ones, they will ultimately be the best ones for us. I never could have believed that had I not experienced that knowledge directly from the Light-God, and then afterwards, had the time to reflect upon the tragic-"appearing" experiences in my own life. They were needed, and I am grateful they happened!

Another thing to remember is that, no matter how much

we may desire something and how much effort we bring to that desire, if it is not part of our destiny, it won't materialize. I may want to win the Power Ball Lottery with a jackpot of billions of dollars, and I may have unshakable faith that I will win it. I may go through my days visualizing winning it; I may speak daily affirmations. But if being rich is not my destiny, then no matter how hard I pray, meditate, will it, believe it, it will not happen.

We are not here for God to serve self by fulfilling every whim, desire, or dreams we may have. We are here to be of service to the Light-God, becoming a vessel of Divine Love to others – no matter how difficult.

Q. Is there a reason for everything?

A. Oh yes, indeed, there is a good reason for everything. I don't bother to get into that mode of thinking however. It's enough for me to know the reason is a good one. That's all I need to know. My Great Teacher, the Light-God, taught me that we are here on this earth plane to learn how to love one another unconditionally, to develop Christ-consciousness, and to use our gifts and abilities to help others. We made an agreement with God, prior to our birth, what lessons we wanted to learn while here on earth.

The soul knows what the human being is supposed to do while here. The soul will bring to the human being the life experiences it will need in order to grow accordingly. So, while the intellect is frazzled at the whole thing, the soul is calmly steering the human in the right direction all the time. Every life experience, every frustration, *everything* has purpose. Nothing is coincidental.

I don't *consciously remember* anything about reincarnation during my experience, and I don't want to imply that I know if reincarnation is true or not. But karma makes good sense to me with regard to the reasons we chose to come to earth in the first place.

The more we learn to draw closer to the Divine Presence within, the more Spirit can help us through this maze of life, and the freer we will become of the bonds that confine us. Spirit desires to experience life through us, to guide us, replenish us, and prosper the purpose for which we are here on earth.

Q. Does God hear my prayers? I try so hard, but I don't get any answers. What gives?

A. Prayer is communing intimately and directly with God. I was taught during my experience that prayer is one of the most powerful energies in the universe – the first being love.

You bet God has been hearing your prayers! I was astonished to learn during my experience that our Beloved Creator knows each and every one of us so intimately. It is so overwhelming for me to realize that with billions of people on this planet, that you and I and everyone, is valued and cherished beyond measure. At times, when I think about this, my mind cannot fathom it. It is like trying to comprehend the vastness of the universe and imagining how far billions of light years away another solar system is located. At some point, the mind shuts down, for it can't conceive of something that vast, that expansive.

In the same way, with billions of people on this planet, we think we are such a small speck of humanity, that surely, the Creator can't possibly notice little old me in my small town, U.S.A. As astounding as it may seem, our Creator knows exactly who we are and where we are at every moment. It is inconceivable to ponder this, just as it is in imagining how large our universe is within many other universes. But I was sent back from the Light-God to help others realize how cherished each and every one of us are – no exceptions. So yes, God is deeply aware of us, and hears our prayers, laughs with us, and sees our tears. We are never alone.

But when you pray, do you believe that God should answer all your prayers? All I can tell you is that no one has the mind of God and no one knows *how* God will work in people's lives. That role is exclusively up to God to determine – not people. I just know that we need to always stay close to God in prayer, in our thoughts, in our hearts, in our songs, and in our actions. The rest will follow as it will. God knows us better than we know ourselves, and knows what is best for us. Having patience and surrendering to allow Spirit to work out the plan for our lives will bring us the peace to understand that all is and will be well.

Pray often, not only for yourself, but for others as well.

Q. God feels so distant to me. I want a close relationship, but how do I accomplish this?

A. My best advice is to pray as if you are a small child who needs your Heavenly Creator's Hand to guide you. Or get mad at God and tell Him with your whole heart that you need him to respond to your needs. Don't settle for anything less. Just as I did that day when I fell on my knees sobbing that I needed God to help me write the book I was told to write. If you forgot, go back to chapter one and review it. Or, continue reading this. Keep pestering God that you NEED Him to ignite the spark of Light within that will illuminate your experience of Him within. Be as sincere as you possibly can and just let go of every reason why you shouldn't do this. Let God have it with both barrels and let Him feel your agony in wanting a deeper relationship with Him. Come to Him with all your guards down. Empty yourself wholly of all preconceived thoughts. Just let God know how much you need Him and want a deeper relationship with Him. Let God be the catalyst for your journey toward Him. Just between you and God – period. How you do this will be up to you.

Q. All this sounds like too much work. I feel like giving up.
A. This life of ours is not merely to show off the products of our intellects and abilities, but to evolve our very souls. We must develop capacities whereby we can recognize reality, and introduce, in the state of life in which we find ourselves, the work that is not made of perishable material but of eternal reality. Let what may happen in the physical world; the soul which has found reality, which is capable of understanding that true values can never be overwhelmed or destroyed.

Don't be discouraged, for though the way to reality is long and laborious, it is a glorious road all the same. The purpose for which we are living spells the liberation of humanity from the prison of ignorance and matter. We aid in the fruition of Spirit by the countless manifestations which we bring through our gifts and our own soul growth.

It is never a hopeless and futile adventure to seek for the Light, for every difficulty you clear away is so much gained. Your Light burns so much brighter when, every so often, you trim the wick from your mind's candle.

Remember, you will have your life review, and it will show you what lessons you gave up on and didn't complete. You will discover, with regret, those areas of growth which should have been well under way before you left the earth life.

I have endeavored to show you the road to true happiness. Why not start or continue your journey now? The way is hard, but it is worth all the trouble, all the discouragements;

for it leads to the discovery of reality and your soul's Divine Rights. When you have reached this point of acceptance, you will find inner peace.

Remember, we came into this world knowing we would experience the ups and downs of life in order to learn important lessons. Whether it be sickness, poverty, abuse, or bad relationships, we knew what we were getting ourselves into. If the road ahead is rocky…it is going to be a bumpy ride.

However, if we can see that every life experience, is to be considered a gift to accelerate our spiritual journey, then we can begin to feel gratitude for the lessons learned. There is no need to fight against it. We just need to heal our ego by forgiving ourselves and by teaching our ego to accept the truth about ourselves and live from that truth.

11

LIFE GIVES TO US JUST WHAT WE BRING TO IT

My Beloved,
Small acts of kindness are huge spiritual gifts that you
lovingly give to others on My behalf. Small acts of
deception, however, are unloving selfish acts stemming
from your ego's need to place yourself above Me. It is
very harmful to your spiritual growth to deceive others,
no matter how small you think the deception might be.
Always be true to yourself and to others my dear child.

What attracts us to some people and not to others? I believe
that it is the radiant soul, a breath of God freely manifesting
it in a human being that we respond to. Once we see the
free soul, living, breathing of Spirit, we are drawn to it like
a moth to light. It is like a flowing forth of Spirit which
permeates all that it contacts.

In our world, we are accustomed to seeing pretense and
deceitfulness. Half the troubles in life come from lack of
Spirit – the honest, genuine and loving reality. Living as
we do, we see the outward semblance, the masks worn by

friends and enemies alike. Moreover, we often have a cloud of emotions, lingering because they are repressed and not expressed. Thus, we become surrounded by a fog of falsity and live in a state of doubt and insensitivity. Our moments of union with the Spirit are few and our shining hours nil.

I know a woman who had so much to give, but never gave. At present, she is a woman soured on life, blaming everybody but herself for her melancholy. In reality, it is her own selfishness to blame. She allowed her personality to get out-of-order and she never fixed it. Her ego was so overdeveloped that she used life without regard for other people. Good never comes from allowing ego to run riot. All beauty of character is lost.

Soul, as I pointed out earlier, is the great evolving Self, blossoming, fruiting the higher personality, its oneness with the Divine Presence within. The person whose soul is being outwardly expressed is one who sings its melodic song of joy. They sparkle, and their presence chases away gloom and inspires us to go joyfully along with them. Where they lead, all follow; when they smile, all smile; and they are always ready to stimulate us and quench our thirst by sharing with us all they have.

The art of living is a fine art, and unless we manifest something of that art in our lives, we are limiting our understanding of the spiritual reality. People should learn to use their soul nature to develop that magnetic personality that will inspire others. If we have a great enough desire, then we can become pretty much what we want to be. Learn to like people. Look for the best in people. Find out what they are interested in. Help people reach their full potential. Catch them doing something right and then compliment them. Be friendly to others by giving them some particular little courtesy. Everyone wants to feel as if they are appreciated, so let that person know you recognize and appreciate their work, their abilities. Treat others according to the Golden Rule: "*Treat others as you would like to be treated.*"

Everyday life is attached to duties, happy or unpleasant. The people who understand how to listen in on their spiritual consciousness realize what is essential and of real value. Let me explain. When someone has evolved spiritually, they have a better understanding of the meaning of love and the *power* of love. It is the life force that can be drawn upon by the individual for his own use, or it can be passed on to others. It is generosity of Spirit that expresses itself in seemingly small but powerful ways. It is a desire to bring happiness to others, to brighten their day and lighten their load.

During my life review, my Great Teacher showed me how relevant those small acts of kindness are. I had no previous idea as to the magnitude of Divine Love they personified. I had no idea that whenever one acts with love, no matter how great or how small, it is the God-Light within that individual that is being released, lifting others, soothing wounded feelings, surrounding fear with healing love. Once the Light-God showed me the importance of those small acts of kindness, I was overcome with remorse when, during my life review, I was shown those times when I failed to give someone a compliment, or when I took someone's service to me for granted, or when I failed to give reassurance to someone.

The virtues of kindness, respect, consideration, and gratitude for all, including oneself, are powerfully transforming. When one seeks to uplift others, we are uplifted in the process. Every kind thought or smile is therefore spiritual and benefits oneself as well as all the world. Love is the magic catalyst that lifts the human self, a drawing upward into the Divine, and a realization that all are one in the Light of God.

Here are a few examples of how a small act of kindness can become very meaningful to someone without our realizing it. Something so small of an event will, upon one's life review, be understood to be such an important act in the context of our spiritual development as to shine as brilliantly as the sun. I cannot stress how significant and of great magnitude these little events have upon our life review when we cross over to the other side. You will see every opportunity you missed when you should have given your love to someone through a small act of kindness and failed to do so. Every single moment of your life will be revealed to you – everything! Trust me, it can be a very painful life review. So I am telling you this because I want to encourage you to **live your life review now! Learn this important lesson now!**

A SMALL ACT OF KINDNESS

My morning started as usual, waking up at 6:00 am. I could hear the six wild Mallard ducks outside squawking and patiently waiting for me to feed them, as I did every morning under the bird feeder. Velcro, my cat, was next on the chow line. His constant meows meant he was serious about eating and he meant business. I came next. Black coffee to wake up my numb, foggy brain was a high priority before I did anything else. *The fish in the pond can wait awhile before I will feed them*, I thought.

About an hour after waking up, I fixed myself one piece of bacon and ate about one-fourth of a cup of chicken salad from the refrigerator. That was it. I was on the Atkins diet. It is very restrictive in its initial phase, and it severely limits carbohydrates. Protein is the basis of the diet. The elimination of carbohydrates puts the body into a condition known as ketosis, in which the body burns the fat stores as energy rather than burning the carbohydrates which turn into glucose for the available energy.

My plan for the morning was to do some shopping errands around 9:00 am, so I got off to an early start expecting to be home by noon. But with all the errands I was doing, I lost track of time. It was 3:00 pm and I hadn't eaten anything more since breakfast than that small amount of chicken salad, or drank anything more than my one cup of coffee. My stomach growled as I was putting the six, twenty-five pound bags of salt into my shopping cart for my water softener at home. I began to feel a bit light-headed, shaky, and weak.

I need to drink some water and eat something, I thought. But the water fountain was on the other side of the grocery store, a rather far walk.

I can wait until I get home, I thought. But I knew that I needed to eat something quickly. *My blood sugar level must be low, or perhaps I am dehydrated,* I thought. I was in close proximity to the deli in the grocery store where I had been shopping, so I glanced at all the hot items for sale in the deli case. Everything in the hot steaming display case was breaded and deep-fried. There were greasy vegetables and chicken, macaroni and cheese, and mashed potatoes, but I was not supposed to eat those foods on my diet. I spotted some chicken that did not appear to be breaded or deep-fried, so I asked the clerk if it was baked. If it was, I could eat a few pieces. I was relieved that there was something I could eat which wouldn't interfere with the diet program I was on.

"*Yes,* the woman said. "*They are our baked fire chicken.*"

"Does that mean they are spicy, hot?" I asked her.

"Yes," she replied.

"I can't tolerate spicy foods; they don't agree with me. I guess I will pass on everything because I also can't eat anything that is breaded," I told her.

Silently I accepted that I wasn't going to be eating anything until I arrived home. But I was so hungry and light-headed because I hadn't eaten or drank anything since early that morning. I was just chit-chatting with the clerk, that's all, when something unexpectedly happened.

"You must eat something!" she insisted.

"Here, let's see, you need to eat some of these potato wedges, and here, you must eat a few of these mozzarella sticks," she said as she carefully pulled them from their hot trays and put them on a napkin for me.

"You must eat! She once again exclaimed. *We'll just call these "samples" to taste,"* smiling at me and placing them in my hand."

"I will also give you a cup so you can go around the corner of the deli where the beverages are located and fill the cup with some water. There is a seating area for you to sit down, rest a bit, and enjoy your food."

How did she know how I was feeling? I didn't mention that to her or give her any indication that I had great thirst or that I was in immediate need of food. With almost a sense of urgency in her voice, she just kept insisting that I must eat something! I told her how appreciative I was of her loving act of kindness, and she responded by giving me a huge, warm smile. She then went back to her work behind the deli counter.

As I was heading toward the seating area where I would fill my glass with water, I began to think. *"The food she gave me is not on my diet. If I eat it, it will get me out of ketosis and*

I won't be burning up my fat reserves. I better throw it away when I go to the seating area and just drink the water." That was my plan.

As I was filling my cup with ice cubes and water, I suddenly realized how unusual it was for someone to give so much food and water like that for someone she didn't know. I'm sure she doesn't give free food like that to everyone who stops by that deli case to choose what they want to purchase. I don't think I looked like a bag-lady, in dire need of food and water. I was just like everyone else in the store going about the business of grocery shopping. Yet, somehow she knew I needed food and water, and pronto! But how did she know?

Soon, a voice in my head made everything very clear to me. It was a teaching that was placed in my heart when I was in the presence of the Light-God during my near-death-like experience many years earlier. I was taught by my Great Teacher, that the smallest acts of kindness that people do for one another are the greatest acts, spiritually speaking. Those small, random acts of kindness are acts of great love that come from the Source of one's Being, the Divine Presence within. Our ego is not involved. We aren't looking for a pat on the back, or anything in return. We simply respond from our heart because it's the loving and right thing to do.

I can't begin to tell you how stunned I was to learn that lesson during my own life review. You will comprehend that as well during yours. Learning that all those little simple and uncomplicated gifts you gave to someone, that you considered to be no big deal, will stand out before you to be the shining example of your soul's character.

The Holy Spirit opens the heart of someone to benefit another through the Divine Love that is within that individual, intuitively guiding that person to help someone else. The heart of that deli clerk was called to open herself to a perfect stranger so that I might receive some nourishment that I needed at that precise time.

Our Divine heritage is a supreme gift to grasp, hold, practice, love, and share. It unfolds its expression through our human selves that brings joy not only to ourselves, but to the One who is joyous in giving it to us.

I stood at that water dispenser pouring the water in my cup, and I knew that I had received a message from the Holy One working through that deli clerk. All things were made clear for choice and understanding. Yes, I needed food and water for my physical body. But I also knew that the One who loves me beyond human comprehension was aware of my bodily needs and wanted to provide for me. I felt blessed and grateful that in the tiny space of my world, inside an ordinary grocery store, my Great Teacher was revealing Himself to me through a deli clerk who opened her heart and offered to help me, unaware that I needed help.

Did I throw away the food she lovingly gave to me? Absolutely not! I realized how vain I had been to be more concerned about losing weight than to be nourished properly. Every morsel of food I ate became a holy experience in which my heart and soul felt the presence of God with me. My physical and spiritual worlds became one in those moments and I left being reminded that God's enfolding power of love is everywhere, in everything, in everyone, and in every situation.

While leaving the grocery store, I asked God to bring that clerk a very special blessing for the very simple, yet special love she gave to me in the form of food and water. Her special blessing will be revealed once she has her own life-review at the end of her earthly life, and she will then understand how her simple act of kindness meant so much to a perfect stranger. She may also get to see how her simple act of kindness was one day written up in a book so that others would be encouraged to open that part of their Divine Self to provide a blessing to someone in the form of a small act of kindness.

The subtle signals are waiting to be noticed from within the heart of our soul, presenting us with opportunities to experience our world and each other from a slightly higher perspective, where the Sacred and the everyday intersect. May each and every person begin to realize how spiritually significant these small acts of kindness are. If you don't realize them now, you will most certainly realize them during your life review. You will see at that time whether you acted on those opportunities that were presented to you, or if you simply turned away and did nothing. Trust me, it can be extremely painful to bear witness to how you related to others while living your life on earth. Yes, even those small moments you didn't think mattered. They do matter, as you will one day find out. I would encourage you to become a small-acts-of kindness person in your corner of the world – every day. You will be increasing your spiritual vibration as you do this, preparing yourself for your ultimate journey to the Light.

ALL DOGS WILL GO TO HEAVEN

Did you ever wonder about synchronicity and how it appears when least expected? Some events can change lives, while others can bring hope and peace. The universe is always reflecting its love for us, but often times, we fail to recognize the many moments it is calling us to receive and to respond to that love.

One day, I decided on a whim to go shopping, something I hadn't planned on doing, but you know how it is, you go, not even realizing why. The weather was hot and my air conditioner had gone out a few weeks earlier, so I figured at least I would stay cool shopping in air-conditioned stores. At least that was my reasoning for going shopping.

After several hours of window shopping without buying anything, I was ready to go home. But on my way out of the store, I spotted a discounted sales area of various items priced 50% to 75% off. Well, being a woman who loves a good sale, my feet automatically went over to the area to check things out. I found some metal garden signs that you label your flowers or vegetables with, and you insert them into the ground to identify your plants. I snatched all fifteen of them, delighted that I found such a good sale.

I chose a check-out lane from the over twenty check-out lanes and placed the garden signs on the counter for the cashier to ring up. She picked up one of the signs and said how lovely it was and asked me what I was going to do with it. I told her that I was going to use them as grave markers in our pet cemetery, and paint the names of our pets on them. I said,

"Most of the little white wooden crosses that dotted the pet cemetery had deteriorated due to weathering, and these metal signs will hold up much better."

She thought that was such a great idea, and then she told me her story about her deceased dogs.

"When I was younger and living at home, our dog died and my father told my brother and me to bury the dog in the back of the shed. He was very specific about the spot to bury the dog. When we started to dig the grave, we discovered the bones of our German Shepard dog who had died some years earlier. We told our father what happened, and he was irate that we dug

up the dog's bones. Wrong spot! So we dug another grave site for our dog."

She then asked me if I bury our dogs in plastic bags.

I said, "When our dogs were at the end-stage of their lives, I always held our dog in my arms while the vet injected the lethal dose. I always wanted our dogs to know they were being loved during their transition. The vet wrapped the dog in an old bedsheet and carried our dog to my car. When I got home, my son would dig a grave and then the two of us would place our dog, wrapped in the bedsheet, into a plastic bag and buried it."

I could see tears welling up in her eyes, so I decided I answered her question and wouldn't talk more about it. But she wanted to tell me more, so I listened. She said,

"When I left home and had a dog of my own, he died after 13 years. I buried him in a plastic bag. But ever since I did that, I have been very distressed. I worry constantly that his soul cannot get out of the plastic bag. It just tears me up thinking about it."

Instead of not saying anything, I decided to tell her that her dog's essence exited his physical body the instant he died. She seemed surprised and I knew I had to explain why I know this. I said,

"Many years ago, I died during childbirth and woke up in the morgue. The instant I died, my soul lifted out of my physical body and entered another dimension with God. I returned to life again to help others understand that we are eternal beings – animals as well, and that we are all loved unconditionally."

I continued,

"When death occurs, there is nothing, no barrier, no obstacle, that will keep a soul from moving on to the next realm. We transition instantly, faster than the blink of an eye. Your dog transitioned as quickly. That plastic bag couldn't keep his essence from going to God."

I told her that I had written 4 books already, and I have given talks around the country on this subject so she could feel more confident of what I was telling her.

"*When my husband was dying in the hospital,*" I continued, "*he was semi-conscious and had his hand raised above his head moving in the air. I asked him what he was doing, and he said, "I'm petting our dogs; don't you see them?" he asked me. "Look, here's Chinook lying next to me, and here's Buffy. Over there is Tasha, Sandy, and Autumn." With a chuckle in his voice, he said, "There's even a turtle here with me."*

My eyes tearing up a bit, I told the cashier, "*You see, all those pets were our deceased pets who came to my husband as he lay dying. He was surrounded with great love and peace as he made his transition to the next realm, and I was given the gift of having been a participant in witnessing that beautiful event. Although I did not physically see our pets as my husband did, there is no doubt whatsoever, that our beloved pets continue to live on in the afterlife, are still aware of us, and will always love us. Love never dies!*"

She couldn't speak for a few moments, looking directly into my eyes with what seemed to be tremendous relief. I was surprised to see her leave her cash register and walk around the counter to me. She hugged me. Her voice quivering a bit, she said,

"*I believe God sent you to my cash register today to help me heal from the torment I have been feeling about my dog's soul not being able to be released from the plastic bag. How can I ever thank you?*"

I replied,

"*Trust that God has your beloved dog in Heaven with Him and he is being loved beyond measure. Many people who have died and returned back to us tell us they were met by their pets when they crossed over. One day you will see your dog again, and he will greet you with a huge, wet kiss. So release your fear and your guilt in burying him in that plastic bag. He is FREE and lives again!"*

With that, she returned to her cash register, and packed my garden signs in a plastic bag, and I was on my way home.

Once home, I contemplated this remarkable exchange between two people who had never met before. One woman who had a great need to heal from the torment she had been dealing with for so many years, and the other woman – me, who became a messenger of healing love for someone simply by opening my heart to her.

ALL SHE HAD TO GIVE

This story was previously written in my book, *Hear His Voice*, but I wanted to mention it again because it is such a good example of tapping into the power source of Divine Love in action.

The year was 1989, the year our house burned down. We were renting a home in the country while our home was being rebuilt. Every morning after my husband left for work, I would drive to the job site to help the construction crew in whatever manner I could. I stained wood siding; I cleaned up debris, anything to be of help since we had a very limited crew – two men. My husband, two sons, and I considered ourselves crew members as well because we pitched in to help whenever we could. Money was very tight because our insurance coverage did not cover the entire amount of the loss. We had to do a lot of the work ourselves.

One particular morning, it was raining very hard. It was one of those cold, spring downpours that would send shivers through your body if you were outdoors amid the loud thunder and lightning that lit up the April sky.

I was getting ready to leave for the job site when I heard a loud knock on the kitchen door. There stood an elderly woman, perhaps in her late eighties, wearing a tattered blue raincoat and holding a small plastic trash bag on top of her head to keep her glistening gray hair dry. I opened the door and she asked,

"Are you Mrs. Clark, the woman whose house burned down?"

With a curious look on my face, I replied, *"Yes."*

"Well Mrs. Clark, I heard about your tragedy in my church. Although I don't have much, I wanted to bring you something."

Slowly reaching her stiff, arthritic hand into her coat pocket, she pulled out a small metal object and placed it very lovingly into my hand. With a tender smile on her face, she said,

"If you are a woman who likes to sew, then I know you can't sew unless you use a thimble. I want you to have mine."

My eyes gazed down at the small silver thimble that she had placed so delicately in my hand, and I noticed that it was very old. The metal had been worn down in several places, obviously from many years of personal use. Then, quickly, she told me that she had to go because her friend who drove her to my house was waiting in the car and had another appointment.

I grabbed my umbrella that was next to the kitchen door and I walked her to her friend's car.

"Oh, I almost forgot Mrs. Clark, as she walked to the trunk of the car and opened it, *"Can you use these plastic jugs for anything?"*

There were about twenty empty gallon plastic jugs that filled the trunk of the car. I wasn't sure what to do, but I didn't want to disappoint the woman by refusing to take them, so I said,

"Well, I'm sure I can find some use for them."

I took all the plastic jugs from the trunk and put them in the garage. I hugged the woman and told her how much I appreciated the gifts she brought me. As I watched the car drive away into the down pouring thunderstorm, I felt as if my eyes were catching a glimpse of a rainbow that was only shining from within my own heart, sending the glow of love I felt outward from me until I could no longer see the car in the distance.

Now, for a moment, think of the chain of events that occurred that enabled that elderly woman to be a ray of Light to a perfect stranger. First, the so-called tragedy of our house fire touched a part of the Divine Love within her, which enabled her to act in a loving way to someone she didn't know. She had to search through her personal belongings for the item she wanted to give me. I suspect that she offered her prayers for our family in the privacy of her home and in her church. The next step of her spiritual fortitude was leaving the known comfort of her home on a cold and windy stormy day to travel many miles in the country to a house she had never been to before.

Her small thimble was all she was able to offer as a gift to me; yet my gratitude was immense! What did I do with those empty plastic gallon jugs? I saved them in the garage, not knowing what I would do with them. But as spring turned to a hot searing summer, we had a severe drought that threatened to destroy my half acre of flower beds that I meticulously cared for through the years. Our house, which was under construction, was in a rural area with no city running water; we had well water. In order to get water from the well, it needed electricity to pump the water up to the surface. But we had no electricity either, so we had no access to any water whatsoever.

Every morning before I drove to the job site, I filled all those empty plastic bottles with water from the house we were renting and put them in my car. That way I was able to water my plants so they wouldn't die. I was able to keep them alive throughout the summer and fall and into their dormancy phase with the water I transported in all those plastic jugs. Had it not been for this lovely woman giving me all those empty gallon plastic jugs, all my plants would have died because we had no rain all those hot months of summer.

I have never forgotten this lovely woman who acted from the inner stirrings of her heart to help someone in need. She may have thought that her small thimble and plastic jugs were insignificant little things she could offer me, but believe me, what she gave of herself was huge, spiritually speaking, because she expressed herself from her true nature – her Divine nature.

Our house fire gave that woman the opportunity to experience the meaning and purpose of our lives, to express unconditional love to one another!

My heart was bursting inside as I thought of the moment she would return "home" to be with our Creator and have her life review. I could envision her joy, when the scene appears before her, of that rainy spring day when she knocked on my kitchen door and gave me so much more than a tiny thimble and twenty empty plastic bottles. She would understand, only at that moment in union with the Light of God, that the tiny isolated moment with me, a perfect stranger, was a shining example of her life's purpose. It's like the winner crossing the finish line at the Olympics and shouting, "I did it!" How thrilled she will be to discover that she did it! She loved unconditionally! The light bulb will flash deep within her spiritual consciousness as mine did during my experience. So that's what it's all about!

My main message to those reading this true story, is that we are ALL messengers of healing love to someone. Listen to the inner voice within that is trying to get you to open your heart and give your love to someone in need. Just help and love others when the opportunity presents itself! It's so simple.

We are to be reminded that we do have a Creator who knows us intimately and who takes the time to speak to us in ways that are unique to us. Spiritual dreams, for instance, are gifts that come to us to inform, protect, comfort, warn, or heal. Most dreams are random and aren't from God. However, a spiritual dream will always leave a sense of peace and love, an intuitive feeling upon awakening that the dream was, indeed, a spiritual message.

Dreams are our way of shutting down our ego-based, rational-thinking mind. They allow our Spirit-self to listen to the serenity beyond the lineal fields of time and logic. In sharing a dream I had one night, I hope to inspire you to know that we are never alone, even though we may think we are, and that our Great Teacher is constantly aware of us.

GOOD GRIEF

My husband died in 2011 after being with me for over 50 years. Even though I have been at Heaven's door several times and I know what he is experiencing, I was grieving the loss of my soul-mate. When I think of what he is experiencing on the other side, I am extremely happy for *him*, but when I think of my life without him, without those warm days of love, I am sad.

My dream was a very powerful message for me, one in which my heart had found a resting place beyond the haze of my grief. It was a place where my soul was shining brightly, manifesting the rebirthing of joy out of yesterday's pain.

In my dream, a grey-haired man wearing a blue shirt and jeans, was singing a beautiful spiritual song. I was standing near him and listening to his soulful voice as he sang his song. As he was walking toward me, he looked deep into my eyes, and I was sort of hypnotized by them. By that I mean there was something very special about the way he was looking into the very heart and center of my eyes, piercing my very soul with love unspeakable.

He moved away from me, continuing to sing that beautiful spiritual song with others who were standing nearby. Suddenly, the entire group of people moved toward me and so did the man. Once again, he stood in front of me and looked so very tenderly into my eyes. I stood before him transfixed in the unearthly, unconditional love that was emanating from his beautiful eyes.

He asked me if I needed a hug. I said,

"*YES! I need a hug!*"

The crowd of people including the man, encircled me with what felt like a wave of butterfly wings wrapped around me so tenderly. The man and all the people began hugging me, nurturing me with tremendous love. I felt as if I had melted into a love so pure and so comforting, surrounded by my spirit brethren and supported by their love. The sound of the man's voice was as if I had heard the inner sound of all life, the inner music of the flowers and the trees, and the very breath of the earth, rhythmic and beautiful. The man said to me,

"*We are healing your grief.*"

As he spoke to me, I cried with tears of gratitude. The

burden of my grief had been weighing heavily on my heart for so long, and now, those butterfly wings that were hugging me were putting wings on my tears, and carrying them away. I woke up and felt some tears lying on my cheeks. I was lying in my bed with a smile upon my lips and the spark of light shining from behind my eyes.

Who was that man with the beautiful loving eyes that penetrated my soul? Who were those people who felt like butterflies wrapping themselves around me? I believe the man was a highly evolved Supreme Being, perhaps Jesus, or an advanced guide, and the people were angels. They came to me by Grace to help heal my grief so that I would know that we are never alone. There is an unseen realm that we can never comprehend enough to fathom, but it is sheer delight when we pause to notice it.

My dream left me with the experiential *knowing* that I am being watched over with great love and compassion. **We all are!** Perhaps in sharing my story, it will help someone in the quiet of their own heart to know that there is no limit to Divine Grace and the manner in which it comes to us. And when we drift into sleep, we are being held in silent serenity, in the arms of the Divine with great love!

THE STORY OF THE YELLOW ROSES

This is a true story of an after-death communication (ADC) I received from my deceased husband. This story was first published in my book, *Stop Trying to Fix Me: I'm Grieving As Fast As I Can*, and has since been published with my permission in other books and magazines. It is a story that has brought hope to many people who read it. I hope it will do the same for you.

My husband and I were high school sweethearts who fell

in love the instant we met at our high school dance. I can still remember that moment as if it were yesterday. While we embraced each other as we danced to the song, *Melody of Love*, our hearts became one and we were together ever since, that is, until his death separated us.

All throughout our dating days and our marriage, Ched always bought me yellow roses for special occasions. Yellow roses are my favorite flowers.

The date was April 28, 2012 which would have been our 50th wedding anniversary, had he lived. We had plans on renewing our wedding vows on that day, but his death one year earlier prevented that. But loving him as I did, I decided to keep my promise to love him for eternity, a vow that honored a lifetime of the love I have for him.

I prayed that Ched would bring me a sign for our 50th wedding anniversary date. The following story is the answer to my prayer.

I have a dear friend who lives in New Jersey who I never met but I love her very much. Her name is Josie Varga. She is an author who is interested in sharing the good news about after-death communications (ADC's) and life beyond death. Since we are both authors interested in the same subject, we often email one another and have become dear friends.

About a week before our anniversary date, Josie emailed me and asked me for my mailing address, as she wanted to send me something. I replied to her email and gave her my address and didn't think much of it. Later that week, I emailed her about something and happened to mention that Ched and I would have celebrated our 50th wedding anniversary in a few days, had he lived.

April 28th was a very emotional day for me. I had been praying for a sign from Ched, a sign that he was still aware of me and loving me. I browsed through our wedding album, admiring how youthful we looked as we began our new life together as man and wife. I think I recalled every detail of that day so I would never forget it. We had promised to love and care for one-another until "death do us part" and now that reality had come to pass. I cried so many tears because I missed him so much. I cried because we were unable to renew our wedding vows like we had planned to do. I just cried and cried.

All the memories of the past were pouring into and out from the hole in my heart. Yet I knew Ched was okay. Because of my heavenly experiences, I knew he was filled with love, joy, and peace unspeakable, yet it did not soothe the raw emotion of the pain that separation had created for me. I ached to receive a message from him – anything!

I called out to him in my anguish. "*Ched, where are you? I need to know you are with me on our anniversary. I need you to bring me a message. Please bring me a message to comfort me. Please bring me a message! God, please allow Ched the ability to bring me a message,*" I shouted.

But the day was coming to a close. It was 5:00 P.M. already and nothing had happened.

Knock, knock. Someone was at the front door. I had been infected with a lung virus for several weeks and I looked like a distressed hag, but I answered the door. A very handsome young man in a beautiful navy blue suit was carrying an arrangement of thirteen beautiful long-stemmed YELLOW ROSES in a vase of water! As he handed the yellow roses to me he said, "Happy Anniversary."

I was anxious to see who sent those beautiful yellow roses to me so I quickly read the card.

It said: "*Dear Nancy, these roses are not from me; they are from Ched. Happy anniversary with all his love. I heard a voice telling me to buy you yellow roses. Please call me and I will explain. Love you, Josie."*

I broke down sobbing from happiness that filled every crevice of my heart. I immediately called Josie and she explained that one day she heard a voice in her head telling her to "*Buy Nancy yellow roses.*" She said it stunned her. "Why?" she wondered. She had no idea why she was supposed to buy me yellow roses, someone she never met before! She told her husband about the voice in her head telling her to "*Buy Nancy yellow roses,*" but she didn't understand why she should do that. She asked her husband what she should do, and he told her to go ahead and buy them. So the next thing Josie did was to email me and ask me what my address was. She didn't tell me at that time why she wanted my address, and I didn't ask.

Remember, Ched contacted Josie to tell her to buy me yellow roses **before** she knew my anniversary date was coming up. She listened to that voice in her head and made a decision to buy them for me without knowing why. She never met me and never met Ched. It was several days after she asked me for my address that I told her of the upcoming 50th wedding anniversary!

I can only imagine how Josie must have felt when she realized that Ched's spirit had contacted her about the yellow roses before she even knew about the important anniversary, and how much I had been wanting to receive a message from Ched.

It was forty-five degrees outside on that cold, rainy day in April. Even though I had a bad virus, I donned a warm coat and gently pulled one long-stemmed yellow rose from the arrangement Josie sent. I gathered Ched's photo, my heart-shaped necklace that contains some of Ched's ashes, his wedding ring, my Bible, and a new ring that I would use to renew my vow to love him for eternity. I walked to the memorial garden my son and I had created for him, and I sat on the bench seat under the white birch tree that he loved so much. The wind whistled through the tall ash trees and the chilly mist perched on my eyeglasses, but I was warmed by the love I was feeling for Ched and for the sign he brought me on our Golden Anniversary to let me know his love was and is still with me.

Before I left, I thanked God for the amazing gift I received that day knowing that love never dies, and that even in death, there is a way for our loved ones to touch our lives in a way that defies our understanding. The universe is filled with love and when we tap into it, we become transformed by it. I know that happened to me that day.

What makes this message from Ched so awesome is that he was a full-blown skeptic on the subject of life after death. Before he died, I told him to be sure and bring me a message from the other side. His eyes rolled up and his nose twitched the way he always did whenever I talked about life after death. He responded by saying,

"If there is no life after death, then I won't be able to bring you a message, and then you will be wrong and I will be right."

I replied, *"You will see that you will live again after you die, so be sure to bring me a message."*

Well, I think we now know who was right and who was wrong. I'm so happy that he found out for himself that life after death exists and that he was able to bring me that message after all in a way that was especially meaningful to me through those yellow roses that he always gave me.

The moral of this story is that love never dies. Love between souls who share a physical life together continues to exist after death, only in a different manner. The mystery of the afterlife cannot be fully understood, only welcomed into the sacredness of the human heart, where it can continue to nourish and instill the *"peace that passeth all understanding."*

In the meantime, I will continue to write and speak to witness to the mystery of the unseen, in the hope that others will be inspired to understand that there is more to our reality than meets the eye. When we are ready to embrace that awareness, the universe will open to us and bring us what we seek.

SO I CAN TELL

My book had been completed and I was ready to send it off to my publisher, when I received an email from a woman who wanted to share her spiritually transformative experience with me for my next book. When I read her story, I knew I had to include it in this book because it is a beautiful testimony coming from a humble heart putting herself in God's presence and sharing with Him what she was feeling and suffering. I am including her entire story as it appeared in the message she sent to me. She wrote:

"This happened about a month after praying for God to reveal Himself. I had been single for about 9 years after my divorce from a very unhappy situation. Learning to live alone and being single was very traumatic for me during the first few years. Over time, I built a new life and began to travel during the summers. After several year, I began to feel intensely lonely and started dating pretty aggressively in order to meet someone. For several years I dated but these relationship prospects turned out to go nowhere. Worse, I seemed to meet men that were cruel and very self-centered. No matter how hard I tried to be attractive, fun, and a real friend, I was continually treated like I was worthless.

Over time this treatment started to impact my self-worth. I started to spiral into anxiety and depression about the prospect of ever finding someone and soon a feeling of doom started to settle within my soul. I felt hopeless and extremely lonely. I truly felt doomed to a fate of loneliness as if a curse was put upon my life. Everywhere I looked, everyone else had someone to love, while I was always turned away if not thrown away. I was continually passed over by the men I wanted.

On numerous occasions they never called back and I couldn't find a reason. Then I met Jon and started getting to know him. He was funny and adorable. A loving man who cared about me and we connected very strongly. For about a year we were always together and every encounter was full of laughter and caring. I fell madly in love.

One day, he too, decided not to call me back for unknown reasons. I never got an explanation or even a hint of any kind. This was the straw that broke the camel's back and I fell into the worst depression I have ever experienced. I would describe it as a pit of hopelessness.

For the first time in my life I lost my will to live. I didn't know this could happen to me. Essentially, I lost all hope in the human race and had nothing to live for. Life made no sense, had no point except to destroy all my ideals about truth, love, honesty, commitment. I remember just falling to my knees and crying out to God. I was wailing and yelling, in the fetal position clutching a pillow.

It went something like this. I was crying and saying I can't do this anymore. I can't take the pain. I told him that if HE didn't exist, I didn't want to go on living. That the world was evil, that people threw you away for no reason, that human beings were self-centered and dishonest. You can't trust anyone. I had to believe that there was a God of Love who was not like that. I told Him that the world says that He doesn't exist and that I'm confused and can't be expected to "have faith" in a book that didn't make any sense. I don't know who to believe. I begged Him to please exist. I told Him I've had all I can endure and have nothing left.

Over the next few weeks my sister pushed for me to see a therapist. She was very worried about how I was feeling, and suggested anti-depressants. I struggled to get up in the morning and prayed daily for strength to a God I knew was not out there.

One night, after work, I started searching for near-death experience accounts on Youtube. A few full video documentaries popped up and I began watching them. I lay there like a wet rag, no energy, no life, no hope, watching with tears in my eyes. Tears because these testimonies offered hope. I clung to these testimonies like a rope dangling down into a pit.

These people said that God did exist. They saw Him. Their descriptions were very convincing and I wanted to believe them. I don't recall how many nights I did this, but then one night, as I lay on the couch listening to testimonies of near-death experiencers, something hit me out of nowhere. I was laying on the couch, depressed and tired. I stared lifelessly at the screen with no thoughts of my own.

Suddenly, it felt like a torrent of a river flowing through me and it went through my chest, out of some place I couldn't detect beyond my chest. It was flowing through me like a river, through the middle of my chest. It was a huge, powerful stream of love. It had a million strands of every kind of love you've ever experienced. For instance, the love of a parent for an infant or the unconditional acceptance of someone who doesn't judge. It loved me so much. It filled me with peace I've never known. And it was unconditional.

Would a mother judge her infant for spilling cereal all over the floor? Neither could God ever judge me for any of my actions. This surprised me very much. The strands of love, the types of love most of them I've never felt before, the variety was endless.

It went through me for about 10 seconds or so. When dissipated, I found that I had a huge smile on my face, which surprised me. I don't smile easily, and there I lay with this enormous grin on my face. Afterwards, I just lay there in shock and disbelief. God had answered my prayer. Essentially saying to me that He existed.

For the next few weeks I was in jubilant shock and disbelief. I kept recounting this experience in my mind, and about a year and a half later, still do so every day. I thank God for His mercy because He gave me a very special hand up so that I would have hope. I was important enough to Him to come down from Heaven and be touched by Him. This amazes me every day.

Since then I've told some people about this. People don't believe you. I also started going to different churches to be with believers of any faith after that. I wanted to be in a spiritual environment of any kind, ordered tons of NDE books, and continue to read them almost daily.

I joined a non-denominational church and was told the whole congregation about my experience when the microphone was being passed around one morning. The topic was how God had helped you in your journey. People stared at me in confusion, but the pastor gave me a warm smile of acceptance. No one approached me though, and I understand that it's far-fetched what I'm describing and doesn't fit Biblical scripture.

Since my experience, my depression is permanently gone. I have God, who else do I need? I used to have an extreme fear of dying. I used to lay awake at night being afraid and thinking about how horrible death was. I am very existential by nature and think deeply on these things.

I'm not thinking about death much anymore except as a blessing because we will be with our Father where our home is. So that fear is gone too. I had a cancer scare about a year ago, and although I didn't want the cancer, surprisingly, I adopted an attitude of curiosity about it. I wondered what God had in store. I wasn't terrified.

Now I'm searching for my purpose because I love God. He's my Father. Nor am I so depressed when people die. I don't believe we are earthly and end our existence here on earth. I know for a fact that isn't true. I am trying to learn to walk like a toddler in this world. To learn to walk means to learn to hear God directing your steps."

Submitted by Kashia; teacher; San Francisco Bay Area, CA

This whole spiritual world is indeed, mystifying. That is why it is essential to open our hearts to the Divine Presence within, for Spirit knows where to lead us. Divine Spirit within will gently and carefully lead us so we will not be broken or get lost along the way, healing the wounds of the past so we can be lifted from the tensions of the seeming problems and into complete love.

12

A FINAL THOUGHT

My Beloved,
Wake up sleepy child. Morning has broken through the
veil of darkness and I am calling you to be the Light
in your little corner of the hurting world with My Love
today. Wake up now!

During fall migration season, I often watch hundreds of geese and other migratory birds flying south, and I wonder what it is in the fall that starts these birds on their long journey. And then in the spring, what starts them to head back North again? Is it some inner urge that whispers timidly at first as the leaves begin to turn? And then does it grow and grow, with the wintry blast, into an overwhelming obsession, until the birds take wing and soar? Or is it only in the leader that the urge to go persuades all the others that now is the time to get up and go? Something so urgent and so irresistible that not a single bird can disregard it. They all fly, as far as they have the strength, toward their destination because of some urge within them.

That's the kind of urge that we need to possess. Something

so overwhelming that we can't resist it. Something that is so genuine that it naturally makes us do the right thing at the right time. It's that unseen something that will not let us take advantage of a weaker person. It's that something that when we are confronted with temptation, compels us to be fair, honest, truthful, and dependable.

There was a definite sense of urgency I felt during my encounter with the Light-God, an urgency for mankind, really. I understood that urgency as being meant for everyone to act upon swiftly – now!

For unless this spiritual life is developed, you will die without realizing the sleeping giants within you. Let those sleeping giants stir and awaken. You cannot climb your spiritual heights without releasing the powers that are within you. It is human to put things off, but Divine to start things off. Never give up until you have released the love that dwells within you, begging to be released and shared with others.

Now is the time to live your life review while there is still time for you to grow more spiritually so that your vibration will be accelerated to enter a higher realm in the afterlife. Please, I beg you, don't turn your back on what I've tried to convey to you in this book. Let the consciousness of the Light be yours to use as a guide, as a feeling of what is right for you. Let it grow in you, for it is through this consciousness that spiritual knowledge is built within. You need this consciousness of the Light as a basis for understanding the teachings given to you.

This supreme gift is your Light–consciousness. Grasp it, hold it, practice it, love it, and share it. Clear your mind at every moment. Live in the here-and-now. The past is dead; let it go. Clear your mind of every negative thought that comes out of the past. Give over all ideas of separation. There is no separation; there is only oneness with the Light-God and with everyone and everything in the universe. You lift and heal others in ways that you are not aware of. Your willingness to be a channel for the Divine brings love onto the earth. If you live a life of love in a deeply divided world, you bear witness to others that it's possible to no longer act out of ignorance or selfishness in ways that cause suffering to yourself and others. **Now** is a time for great love, of great lifting, of great healing through you as a messenger of hope to others.

Let the awareness of the Light in you equalize you with everyone. Though you may ascend to higher consciousness, you remain equal with all as individual expressions of God. There is no high; there is no low. There is no superiority or inferiority. All are equal in God. Therefore, accept this equality-in-life principle in all you do, say and feel.

Know beyond all doubt that the Divine Presence is the reality of your being, and allow it to be brought forth into reality in your life. That, my friends, is the message the Light-God sent me back to share with humanity. I offer it with great love. By accepting it, may you have a foundation of faith to build upon, that brings with it, peace and a stillness so great that you can hear God whispering His Love throughout your Divine Spirit.

There is no need to strive for perfection; just strive to give your love in as many areas of your life as possible, and you will be okay. As Mother Teresa reminds us, "*We cannot do great things on this earth, but we can do small things with great love.*"

Those who love do their best, and forgive the rest.

COMMENT

I receive many comments from people from all around the world who have read my books and who took the time to contact me with encouraging words of praise. While I am deeply humbled by their support of my work, I am most grateful to my Great Teacher, the Light-God, who graced me with this gift and is the One who deserves the glory. I am only the pencil in God's Hand who willingly accepted this calling, this lifetime mission on earth so that the Light will shine into many places and into many lives.

I have come to know with certainty that if we walk with the Light, there is no limit to what we can achieve, or to what we may receive. But remember that always these gifts are to be used for the benefit of others. When we help others, something is set in motion, the power of love comes to its fulfilment! We may not immediately see the good that comes from this flow of love, but we can be sure it is happening.

With his permission, I want to share a personal email I received from a gentleman living in Scotland thanking me for the work I am doing. However, his message is really a message for all of us to appreciate as we move together, helping each person by spreading the Light. It is such a good reminder that those we help are blessed in ways that we may never realize. So I am sharing this man's expression of thanks because I truly feel it is meant for each and every one of us who may not realize the effect we have on one-another. May it help to expand our appreciation of one-another by reminding us what lies within all of us and expressing that appreciation to God and to each other.

"When I read your words-the words of someone who KNOWS that there is a greater Being, a greater perspective – I feel very

satisfied — like a child who has got lost in some amusement park/ house of horrors — got lost with his cotton candy all day and finally finds his home and loving parents. Finding something real amidst a "Pinocchio" nightmare of illusion of uncaring and unlove. Remembering that amongst all the slip-slidey-ness of the world — a real Friend is there when you get home. Those who help us realize that there is stability amongst amusement park con-artists and carnival side-shows."

As the gentleman from Scotland pointed out, when we are lifting others into a greater awareness of their Divine nature, we have a real friend helping us to realize there is stability in growing in spiritual awareness and living the life of love and peace in the midst of seeming confusion. That, my friends, is living the true life.

His letter to me continued with the following metaphor.

"I was talking with my friend about how people that we know cope with existential facts and fears in their lives.

I spoke about my cousin who is diagnosed with OCD and also psychotic illness. He has a ritual about how he locks the door to his house; he does it in sets of 3, over and over again.

I deal with my existential fears by studying death and meeting people who have had NDEs, and studying my own small, mystical experience.

I had the image: as if two people were sitting side-by-side on a haunted-house ride in an amusement park (I have never been on one.)

One person has had a mystical experience in which they KNOW that the soul's life is eternal. The other person has not.

They both scream and get scared, laugh, react…but one knows that it is only a ride, that will be over soon — and that they will come out into the bright sun of a Saturday afternoon.

The other believes that this reality, in the haunted house, is real and will go on forever.

Why I like to 'sit' next to you – in this very real believable world, or ride: I can be reminded that this is only a ride: we paid to get our ticket, we chose to go in and on the ride. I can go through the real experience of fear and loss, and threat, and I will even scream when it gets too hairy – and you will too, but you also KNOW that you might as well enjoy the ride – because it's only a brief ride – one you chose.

That was why I did the conference on expanding conscious-ness and near-death experiences last year- to, in a sense, 'sit' next to you, hold your hand, know you, and learn from you… to begin to stretch my BELIEF into a KNOWING – to know that there is another, much grander, much more loving, much less frightening reality – just outside of my vision – kind of like the curtain, that one sees peripherally at the sides of the stage at a theatrical play – that is a constant reminder that the 'reality', the drama that is happening on that stage, that one gets all emotionally involved in, is really only a play! The actors convince us, but they take off their makeup and go happily home!

Is it like this?

I responded to him and said, *"Yes, it is like this!"*

When the soul and its powers have evolved sufficiently, it is able to recognize wisdom when you see it face to face. Then you will become sensitive to the radiations of light which will clear away the shadows, fill the dark places with illumination, and render it possible for you to get a birds-eye view of life from stunning heights.

"To know the road ahead, ask those who are coming back." Chinese Proverb.

They are our mentors, and they have experienced a more

intense lucidity than what you are trying to accomplish on your own. They lead us and fire our enthusiasm – burning out the dross and enabling us to strike out along many new paths. But we are able to pass on to you some of our ideas and ideals only when you are inwardly prepared to receive. Then, the Light is forthcoming.

For one quiet moment, visualize your heart filled with love and breathe in the breath of God. This love is implanted in your being. Breathe out the blessing of God's heartfelt love calling upon the Power of the Spirit for others. As you allow the power to manifest through you in order that you may help others, so you will receive help, and the more you do in the name of love, the greater will be the inflow.

Do not be reluctant to express your true loving nature. Take each challenge as it comes and be at peace, for the Creator of the universe lives within you. Know that you are progressing always at your perfect right pace. And please….. never think that you fall short and cannot do what you would like to do. God doesn't call the qualified. He qualifies the called.

AN EXERCISE IN LIVING THE LESSONS FROM THE LIGHT

Kenneth Ring, PhD, NDE researcher and Professor Emeritus, University of Connecticut, in his wonderful book, Lessons from the Light that he co-authored with Evelyn Elsaesser Valarino, wrote that "*It is not only possible for persons open to NDEs to learn from them, but to internalize their essential insights and make them their own. In this way, such persons become like NDErs themselves and come to see the world with NDE-mediated vision.*"

I would suggest that this same exercise can also be used

for persons open to the insights from other spiritually transformative experiencers as well.

Dr. Ring suggests taking several hours or even a day to reflect upon some of the teachings that these experiencers have conveyed to us. In essence, you will be "role-playing" the way an experiencer relates to his outer world from his inner world of love and compassion for others. You will be setting an intention for your human life to trust and acknowledge the fullness of who you are. It is suggested to "let yourself experience the world with eyes tender with compassion – for yourself as well as for others."

Dr. Ring suggests that sometimes you will fall out of this role-playing exercise, but remind yourself of what you are trying to accomplish. You are trying to "acquire this gift of the NDE yourself – and in that way, be able to give it, as NDErs do, to others."

The next part of this exercise, according to Dr. Ring, is to write in a journal about "how you felt and what insights came to you." He also suggests that you describe some encounters you had with others in which you were able to act in the manner that reflected what you learned from the way experiencers live their own lives. His next suggestion is brilliant. Dr. Ring suggests that you "look at others from your own point of view, and then imagine what a being of light might communicate to you about them." With his gentle wisdom, Dr. Ring tells us "not to judge your failures, but to learn from them." This is a particularly good way to see how you are progressing as you become aware of your intended practice to become the kind of person you have been reading about.

This exercise is such a wonderful, almost meditative way of transforming one's self to live a life more congruent with our inner Divine nature that I so passionately speak about in this book. By putting into practice the lessons we glean from those who have been on the other side, we will be preparing ourselves for our soul's destiny after death and, at the same time, embracing our heart, the hearts of others, and the heart of life.

While it is true that the Light loves us all unconditionally, it doesn't mean that we can get away with all sorts of bad behavior thinking it won't matter. There are always repercussions to good or bad behavior, both in this life and in the afterlife. The message from the Light I was given to share with humanity is to take individual responsibility for our lives now! Learn to love self and others now, while we are here on earth to learn that lesson. Use the technique that Dr. Ring has described to help you develop your own love, awareness, and choice in this lifetime, so that you will be creating and playing out your own story, from the perspective that many near-death and other spiritually transformative experiencers have taught us.

If I have been helpful to you in some way in getting that message across to you, then hooray! If not, then I would ask that you keep reading books, attending workshops, and listening to experiencers who were granted visitation on the other side of the veil. Perhaps the seed that was planted will one day sprout and you will begin to take seriously this message coming from the mouths of thousands of experiencers, many of whom have stood up against ridicule, and cynicism in order to bring this message to humanity for our collective benefit. Bless their hearts for wanting to unselfishly help others in this way.

Martin Luther King, Jr. once said, "*Everybody can be great because anybody can serve. You don't have to have a college degree to serve. You don't have to make your subject and verb agree to serve. You only need a heart full of GRACE – a soul generated by LOVE."*

Now, I will ask you, "What do you plan to do now with the knowledge you have been given? Will you close this book and return to your life as you know it, or will you open a new chapter in the book of your own life and become an active expression of the Light in your corner of the world? I hope you will make the right decision now, while there is still time."

Writing books is my way of reaching vast audiences with the message of love I was given by the Light to promulgate. I could not, or would not want to do this work without the help of the Light-God. So now, let me tell you a secret I have only shared with a handful of my closest friends.

The day I received the first copy of my first book, *Hear His Voice* from my publisher and held it in my hands was one of the most humbling days of my life. I was holding in my hands the book where all the words that first formed in my mind with the help of God had been brought into physical manifestation.

What do you think most authors do with the first copy of their book hot off the press? I think they probably would set it in a nice place in their home or office, a coffee table, a mantle, or a bookshelf.

Where do you think I placed my first copy of *Hear His Voice?* Well, first of all, I had no ego need to fulfill by displaying my book prominently somewhere in my home. All I wanted to do was to give back to God a gift in return for the gift of actually encountering Him during my experiences, for transforming my life in such a beautiful way, and for helping me to write the book.

So, I immediately inscribed a message in the book of

my heartfelt gratitude to God for the cherished gift He had given to me. I wrapped my book in nice wrapping paper and tied it with a beautiful bow. I placed the book in a plastic bag and went outside and into the woods where I live.

With a shovel, I dug a hole and placed the book into the hole and covered it with dirt. It was a symbolic act to give back to God, in some concrete way, something in return for all He had given to me; it was my gift to Him. It was the book He had asked me to write for Him. I did write it, and I didn't feel it belonged to me as much as it belonged to God.

I prayed for an hour on my knees beside the now covered hole which held my book, and I rededicated myself to serving God in whatever manner He would ask of me. I just poured out my love to God with tears rolling down my cheeks while kneeling there in the forest with the sun streaming down between the tall ash trees. I felt the warmth of God's Love for me, filling every cell of my human body. It was an intense feeling of communion with God-a feeling to this day that I can vividly recall.

I have no idea where that spot is in the woods. But I know it is there. One day when the land is developed with homes, a bulldozer will probably unearth my present to God, unwrap it, and read the inscription I wrote to God. I hope it will fall into the hands of someone who will read it and who will be helped in some way. If not, at least the book will continue to rest buried beneath the soil as a tangible expression of my love for God and my gift to Him.

Every book I have written is my gift to God first, and second, to the world. I pray that those written words will settle into the hearts of those reading my books so that those hearts will be touched by the message that our Creator wishes all to hear. Then, when I return "home" again, and I am asked, "How well did you love? I want to be able to answer that and say, "I did the best I could, mistakes and all, to serve my fellow man, and God." I pray the same for you as well.

*We come from Love; we are sustained by Love,
and to Love we shall return."*

QUOTES TO INSPIRE YOU

"I will love the light for it shows me the way, yet I will endure the darkness because it shows me the stars."

—Og Mandino

"Everyone has inside of him a piece of good news. The good news is that you don't know how great you can be! How much you can love! What you can accomplish! And what your potential is!"

—Anne Frank

"All the darkness in the world cannot extinguish the light of a single candle."

— Francis of Assisi

"The greatest achievement was at first and for a time a dream. The oak sleeps in the acorn, the bird waits in the egg, and in the highest vision of the soul a waking angel stirs. Dreams are the seedlings of realities."

—James Allen

"The smallest deed is better than the greatest intention."

—John Burroughs

"Love rests on no foundation. It is an endless ocean, with no beginning or end."

—Rumi

"I am not afraid of storms for I am learning how to sail my ship."

—Louisa May Alcott

"One of the most tragic things I know about human nature is that all of us tend to put off living. We are all dreaming of some magical rose garden over the horizon instead of enjoying the roses that are blooming outside our windows today."

—Dale Carnegie

"Character cannot be developed in ease and quiet. Only through experience of trial and suffering can the soul be strengthened, ambition inspired, and success achieved."

—Helen Keller

"If you want others to be happy, practice compassion. If you want to be happy, practice compassion."

—Dalai Lama

"We don't see things as they are, we see them as we are."

—Anais Nin

"Too many of us are not living our dreams because we are living our fears."

—Les Brown

"The only person you are destined to become is the person you decide to be."

—Ralph Waldo Emerson

"Kindness is the language which the deaf can hear and the blind can see."

—Mark Twain

"When one door closes, another opens; but we often look so long and so regretfully upon the closed door that we do not see the one which has opened for us."

—Alexander Graham Bell

"You may never know the results of your actions but if you do nothing, no results will be seen."

—Mahatma Gandhi

"Though no one can go back and make a brand new start, anyone can start from now and make a brand new ending."

—Carl Bard

"A problem can't be solved with the same consciousness that created it."

—Albert Einstein

"Find the seed at the bottom of your heart and bring forth a flower."

—Shigenori Kameoka

"When you were born, you cried and the world rejoiced. Live your life in a manner so that when you die, the world cries and you rejoice."

— Native American Proverb

"Twenty years from now you will be more disappointed by the things that you didn't do than by the ones you did do."

—Mark Twain

"I will act as if what I do makes a difference."

— William James

"Love sees roses without thorns."

—German Proverb

"We are made for loving. If we don't love, we will be like plants without water."
— Archbishop Desmond Tutu, Nobel Peace Prize winner

"Life is a mirror, and will reflect back to the thinker what he thinks into it."
—Ernest Holmes

"Happiness is not something ready-made; it comes from your own actions."
—Dali Lama

"Attitude is a little thing that makes a big difference."
—Winston Churchill

"The important thing is not to stop questioning. Curiosity has its own reason for existing. One cannot help but be in awe when he contemplates the mysteries of eternity, of life, of the marvelous structure of reality. It is enough if one tries merely to comprehend a little of this mystery every day. Never lose a holy curiosity."
—Albert Einstein

"The greatest use of a life is to spend it on something that will outlast it."
—William James

"Love is the beauty of the soul."
—St. Augustine

"Truth is by nature, self-evident. As soon as you remove the cobwebs of ignorance that surrounds it, it shines clear."
— Mahatma Gandhi

"It doesn't matter how slow you go as long as you don't stop."

—Confucius

"Death is not extinguishing the light; it is putting out the lamp because the dawn has come."

—Rabindranath Tagore

"Death is not a sinking into nothingness but the beginning of life. Here we walk in shadow there in sunshine; here in strife, there in peace; here in a foreign land, there in the Father's house; here we believe, there we know."

—Bishop Toth

"We make a living by what we get, but we make a life by what we give."

—Winston Churchill

"The greatest gift you can give to others is the gift of unconditional love and acceptance."

—Brian Tracy

"In the midst of movement and chaos, keep stillness inside of you."

—Deepak Chopra

"Know thyself or at least keep renewing the acquaintance."

—Robert Brault

"What seems to us as bitter trials are often blessings in disguise."

—Oscar Wilde

"Everyone is here because he or she has a place to fill, and every piece must fit itself in the big puzzle."

—Deepak Chopra

"It doesn't matter how slow you go as long as you don't stop.
—Confucius

"The life of the body is the soul; the life of the soul is God."
—St. Anthony of Padua

RESOURCES

The International Association for Near-Death Studies, Inc. (IANDS), is a very reputable organization dedicated to the dissemination of information about the research, education, and support of near-death and similar experiences. Its membership is open to everyone. It publishes a scholarly journal, *The Journal of Near-Death Studies*, and a quarterly newsletter, *Vital Signs*, for its members. There are many local chapters in the United States and throughout other countries. More information about IANDS can be had at their website: http://www.iands.org. Email: Services@iands.org

Information about the Columbus, Ohio IANDS group:
http://www.freewebs.com/iandscolumbus
or Email: healeygarden@msn.com

Another excellent online organization is ACISTE (American Center for the Integration of Spiritually Transformative Experiences). This organization supports those who have had a STE with lots of information, articles, research data, and experiencer forums. Go to: http://www.aciste.org for more information.

The world's largest website devoted to near-death experiences is hosted by Jeffrey Long, M.D., New York Times bestselling author, *Evidence of the Afterlife: The Science of Near-Death Experiences* and his wife, Jody Long, JD. The website is: http://www.nderf.org with over a half million readers a month. It is chocked full of valuable information.

Another noted NDE researcher is Kenneth Ring, PhD, Professor Emeritus at the University of Connecticut, considered the premier scientific researcher in the field of near-death experiences and an internationally recognized authority on the subject. Any of his books would be worth reading. They include: *Life at Death; Heading Toward Omega; Mindsight;* and *Lessons from the Light.*

PMH Atwater is another prominent NDE researcher who has contributed so much to the field. Her website http://www.pmhatwater.com is a bountiful site where you can find all her books, information, and additional resources for your interest and sign up for her monthly newsletter. Highly recommended!

The ADC Project formed by Bill and Judy Guggenheim offers information about their research on after death communications (ADCs) from over 3,300 firsthand accounts from people who believe they have been contacted by a deceased loved one. Their book, *Hello From Heaven!* contains 353 such accounts. A must read! Go to http://www.after-death.com

Of course I would highly recommend checking out Raymond Moody's website: http://www.lifeafterlife.com for a complete list of his books and to follow his work.

Eternea.org is very good. http://www.eternea.org. It is a non-profit organization co-founded by Eben Alexander, M.D. and John R. Audette, M.S. It sponsors research and education about spiritually transformative experiences (STEs) and non-local consciousness (NLC).

A great online site is David Sunfellow's NHNE Near-Death Experience Network. www.the-formula.org/. This is where the lion's share of carefully picked, lightning bolt NDE content lives. It is home to David's two main video presentations "How Near-Death Experiences Are Changing the World," and "What Near-Death Experiences Teach Us."

The Institute for Mystical Experience Research and Education, Inc. (IMERE) www.imere.org. IMERE's mission is "To advance the creation, communication, and application of mystical experience knowledge to benefit society and to improve the lives of people throughout the world." You can read about mystical experience accounts, receive its newsletters, and participate in an anonymous research questionnaire if you have had a mystical experience yourself.

The Academy for Spiritual and Consciousness Studies, Inc. www.ascsi.org Its' mission is "to discern, develop and disseminate knowledge of how paranormal phenomena may relate to and enhance the development of the human spirit."

Barbara Harris Whitfield, author, NDEr, and researcher, along with husband, best-selling author and physician Charles Whitfield, M.D., work in private practice helping adults that were repeatedly traumatized as children. Good website. Listing of Barbara's books. www.barbara-whitfield.com.

Josie Varga, author and motivational speaker helps the bereaved by sharing her message that life never ends and love never dies. Check out her website: www.josievarga.com

Larry Dossey, M.D., New York Times bestselling author, is an international advocate of the role of the mind in health and the role of spirituality in healthcare. He has written over a dozen books. A few include: *One Mind; The Power of Premonitions; Prayer Is Good Medicine; Healing Words.* His website is: www.dosseydossey.com

Dannion Brinkley was struck by lightning and had an NDE. His experience is probably the most widely recognized NDE in the world. His New York Times bestselling book, *Saved By the Light* was made into a movie by the same name. Dannion's wife Kathryn also had a near-death experience and together, they are making a huge impact in our world of higher consciousness. Check out their website: www.dannionandkathryn.com

Mark Pitstick, MA, DC, Director of Education for Eternea. org. Author, speaker, focusing on soul issues and spirituality. Excellent newsletter available on his website www.soulproof. com

Other researchers worth Googling include:
Peter Fenwick, M.D.; Bruce Greyson, M.D.; Pim van Lommel, M.D.; Melvin Morse, M.D.; Sam Parnia, M.D.

ALSO BY THE AUTHOR OF REVELATIONS FROM THE LIGHT

Hear His Voice: The Light's Message for Humanity
National Award-winning book

214 pages, soft cover

A breathtaking journey into the Light while the author died. She woke up in the morgue. Years later, another journey into the Light transformed her life forever.

Endorsed by NY Times best-selling author, Larry Dossey, M.D., John White, internationally known author, Kenneth Ring, PhD, and PMH Atwater, both world-renowned near-death experience researchers.

"I've read many books about near-death experiences and spirituality, and Hear His Voice is the best book I have ever read. What makes this book outstanding is the author's sincerity, humility, and love as she takes us on a breathtaking journey into the domain of the Light. It is here where this inspired writing had its effect on my own personal spiritual journey. I am a better person for having read this wonderful book. I highly recommend Hear His Voice!"

—Jason Evans

My Beloved: Messages from God's Heart to Your Heart

National Award-winning book

138 pages, soft cover (Includes a 70 minute CD "God is Closer than We Think) spoken by the author

From a woman who spent 15 minutes in the Eternal Sacred Realm and returned from the heart of God to help people remove their barriers to direct experience of the Divine within.

"The author of Hear His Voice has brought yet another treasure into the world. This book is a stunningly beautiful collection of glimmering spiritual pearls. It picks up where her last book left off, further elucidating the path we all so deeply wish to travel. You'll want to take your time reading through it, because it's absolutely packed with insights. This is one book where nothing is unimportant – nothing. The writing is both beautiful and concise, which places this among the very rarest of written works. Coming through this author, it is my opinion that the words can be trusted fully, and this exceptional book has my very highest recommendation."

—William W. Hoover, M.D.

Divine Moments: Ordinary People Having Spiritually Transformative Experiences

334 pages, soft cover. Also published and translated in Germany as well as USA

Endorsed by NY Times best-selling author, Eben Alexander, M.D., *Proof of Heaven*

The author's 30 years of research went into this book that documents the true-life stories of ordinary individuals whose lives were transformed in ways they could not have imagined. Endorsed by Reverend Howard Storm, best-selling author, My Descent Into Death; Larry Dossey, M.D. best-selling author, Prayer is Good Medicine; One Mind; Yolaine Stout, President, American Center for the Integration of Spiritually Transformative Experiences.

"Near-death experiences (NDEs), have been increasingly embedded in the fabric of our culture over the 36 years since Dr. Raymond Moody coined the term. Nancy Clark had benefited from her first near-death experience beginning 15 years before Dr. Moody's landmark book, Life After Life, and has been studying these profoundly elucidating experiences ever since. With Divine Moments, she presents the poignant and passionate stories of individuals concerning their mystical experiences transcending our earthly realm-without being "near-death." In addition, she offers her deep wisdom concerning the true value of these phenomena based on her extensive life study. All people have access to these same mystical experiences, which can change their lives in remarkably meaningful ways-through prayer, meditation, loving relationships with animals, the "gift of desperation", or just being open to them under the right circumstances, such as living through the difficulties of human existence.

A profound sense of the true mystery of the nature of consciousness has permeated the field of neuroscience and the Philosophy of Mind

over the last few decades. This awareness among scientists and phi-losophers is opening the door to a wider acceptance of the validity of these mystical experiences in the understanding of our existence, and the possibility that mind might exist independently of the brain. The momentum from many different directions is leading towards a fun-damental change in human consciousness, offering hope and peace to a troubled world. Divine Moments provides a keystone to that global conscious awakening, bringing the mystical and the Divine to all of us – in this life!"

— Eben Alexander lll, M.D. Neuroscientist; Author, *Proof of Heaven*

Stop Trying to Fix Me: I'm Grieving As Fast As I Can

143 pages, soft cover

One of the most helpful things we can experience when we are in the midst of grief is to hear the personal story of someone who is working through her grief and beginning to see a glimpse of hope for the future.

"The death of a spouse after a long loving marriage can be and often is devastating to the survivor. It leaves an open wound that cannot be cauterized, and certainly not by formulaic well-meaning words intended either to comfort or to change the subject away from the survivor's unbearable, unrelenting grief. Nancy Clark has had to endure both her grief and the sometimes almost heartless attempts of others to "cure her of her sorrow." This is her moving and searingly honest testimony that shows that while grief may someday at least subside, the love that animates it only grows stronger. Nancy's grief is a kind of sacred remembrance, a way of honoring that love until both she and her beloved can be united again. Why, then should one try to

overcome it? It is not an illness to be cured, but a means of cherishing the unfathomable beauty of an undying love."

—Kenneth Ring, PhD, Psychology Professor Emeritus, University of Connecticut; world-renowned near-death experience scientific researcher; author, *Lessons from the Light*

"*I have lived what Nancy writes about and know that only love is immortal. Because of the difficulties people have dealing with loss and death we are unprepared when it comes into our lives. Only you can fix yourself and heal your wounds and life but Nancy's experience and words can help to coach and guide you through this difficult time.*"

—Bernie Siegel, M.D. Best-selling author, *Faith, hope & Healing*

"*This unique book offers a wealth of information about grief and after-death communication (ADC) experiences. I recommend it very highly to everyone who is providing emotional support to someone who is grieving the death of a loved one. I wish it had been available when many of my family members and friends had died.*"

—Bill Guggenheim, co-author, *Hello From Heaven*!

BOOK ORDERING AND CONTACT INFORMATION

All books are available for purchase on Amazon.com

For autographed copies sent directly from the author, please email Nancy Clark:

nancyclarkauthor@gmail.com for more information

Snail Mail: Nancy Clark

7501 McKitrick Rd, Dublin, OH 43017

If you have enjoyed this book, the author would appreciate it if you would post an endorsement of it on Amazon.com. This is a good way of letting others know about it. Simply go to Amazon.com and click "Write a review" and follow the prompts. Nancy thanks you for your consideration.

ABOUT THE AUTHOR

Nancy Clark is a graduate of Women's Medical College at the University of Pennsylvania, with further training at Mount Sinai Hospital in New York. She is a retired cytologist (study of cells) and has conducted cytology cancer research at a major university. Nancy is an international award-winning author of several books that deal with her spiritually transformative experiences. She has given talks around the country and has been interviewed on radio and television. She is the founder and facilitator for the International Association for Near-Death Studies (IANDS) in Columbus, Ohio since 1984.

Her passion is to inspire others to comprehend the core message of the near-death and similar spiritually transformative experiences with the hope that this will help people learn more of the growth possibilities they provide.

The 23rd Psalm   3/23/1

The Lord is my Shepherd
There is nothing that I lack, (Want
He makes me lie down in
green pastures. He leads me
beside still waters
He restores my soul

He guides me along right paths
for His Names Sake

Yea though I walk through
the Valley of the Shadow of
Death,
I will fear no evil, for
you are with me.
Your rod and your staff they
comfort me.

You set a table before me
in the presence of my enemies,
you anoint my head with oil
my cup runneth over,
Surely, goodness and mercy
will follow me all the
days of my life and
I will dwell in the House
of the Lord forever.

CPSIA information can be obtained
at www.ICGtesting.com
Printed in the USA
BVHW032358270219
541403BV00003B/411/P